'Let wonder seem familiar'
Endings in Shakespeare's
romance vision

'Let wonder seem familiar'

Endings in Shakespeare's romance vision

R. S. WHITE

Humanities Press : New Jersey
Athlone Press : London

First published in the United States of America in 1985
by Humanities Press Inc., Atlantic Highlands, NJ 07716
and in Great Britain in 1985 by
The Athlone Press Ltd., 44 Bedford Row, London WC1R 4LY
Copyright © 1985 R. S. White
'Let wonder seem familiar' is an expanded version of
Shakespeare and the Romance Ending, *privately printed in 1981*

Library of Congress Cataloging in Publication Data

White, R. S., 1948–
'Let Wonder Seem Familiar'
1. Shakespeare, William, 1564–1616—Tragicomedies.
2. Shakespeare, William, 1564–1616—Comedies.
3. Closure (Rhetoric)   4. Love in literature.
5. English literature—Early modern, 1500–1700–
History and criticism. 6 Romances—History and
criticism.   I. Title.
PR2981.5.W5   1984   822.3'3   84–15812
ISBN 0–391–03194–5

British Library Cataloguing in Publication Data

White, R. S.
'Let Wonder Seem Familiar'
Rev. exp. ed.
1. Shakespeare, William—Knowledge—
Literature   2. Shakespeare, William—
Technique   3. Closure (Rhetoric)   4. Romances—
History and criticism
I. Title
822.3'3   PR3037

ISBN 0–485–11256–6

*Typesetting by The Word Factory
Rossendale, Lancashire
Printed in Great Britain by
Paradigm Print, Bungay, Suffolk*

To my Mother and Father

Contents

Preface

The first version of this book was published privately in 1981 under the title *Shakespeare and the Romance Ending* in a limited print-run. It sold out within a year and a continuing demand for copies has led to the present book. I was given confidence by the reception of the former book among academics, students and other readers of Shakespeare to feel that the ideas merited a wider circulation. I have profited also from suggestions and criticisms offered by readers, and it became clear that the book could well be amplified in various places. The ideas remain the same but some sections have been expanded or rewritten. In particular, the special commercial restraints upon the first edition prevented the inclusion of extensive annotation, and it is a pleasure now to have room to pay off some more debts to the many critical works which helped me formulate my ideas in the first place. Unfortunately, however, it is impossible to trace comprehensively the road to Xanadu in any work on Shakespeare, and there remain many other oblique sources for ideas and expressions for which I must remain silently grateful. It is a pleasure, once again to record gratitude to people who helped at various points: Dr John Wilders, Katherine Duncan-Jones, the late J. C. Maxwell, Barbara Everett, Stanley Wells, Susan Dady, Dr Desmond Graham, John McGahern, John Pellowe, Professor Ernst Honigmann, Sally Woodhead, Dr David Norbrook, Ian Robson, the late Dr Peter Laver, Jane Whiteley, and now the many reviewers, correspondents and students who offered advice and suggestions. If I have not in every case agreed with their comments I have certainly heeded them.

R. S. WHITE
1984

I The sense of an ending
in Elizabethan romance

Aristotle found it a straightforward matter to define an ending:

> A beginning is that which does not necessarily come after something else, although something else exists or comes about after it. An end, on the contrary, is that which naturally follows something else either as a necessary or as a usual consequence, and is not itself followed by anything.[1]

In more recent times, writers and critics have found the issue to be considerably more complicated than this, particularly when the poet is striving to convince us that his work is more than a mere artifice and has some mimetic relationship with our perceptions of the real world. D. H. Lawrence, defending free verse, speaks most eloquently of the need to make literature follow the flowing line of life itself, allowing no definitive close:

> The poetry of the beginning and the poetry of the end must have that exquisite finality, perfection which belongs to all that is far off. It is in the realm of all that is perfect. It is of the nature of all that is complete and consummate. This completeness, this consummateness, the finality and the perfection are conveyed in exquisite form: the perfect symmetry, the rhythm which returns upon itself like a dance where the hands link and loosen and link for the supreme moment of the end. Perfected bygone moments, perfected moments in the glimmering futurity . . . But there is another kind of poetry: the poetry of that which is at hand: the immediate present. In the immediate present there is no perfection, no consummation, nothing finished. The strands are all flying, quivering, intermingling into the web, the waters are shaking the moon. There is no round, consummate moon on the face of running water, nor on the face of the unfinished tide.[2]

In the belief that the second part of this passage gives us a modern analogy for the characteristic structural rhythm of romance, while the first part describes something of the comic ending, I shall be to some extent swimming in its wake, attempting to evoke something of the vision or spirit of these related genres. The reader of a scholarly bent will find in the Appendix a more specific summary of what we know about the factual, historical connections between older romance, Elizabethan romance, and romantic comedy. Since the literary quality and effect is often preciously difficult to define, "more flyttinge than the mutabilitie of floures of the somer sesoun",[3] I hope a wider range of reference will be forgiven in the commentary on the plays.

In this book, we shall be examining the intersection in Shakespeare's works of two genres, neither of which strikes one immediately with its mimetic qualities, but more with its controlled artifice. Both comedy and romance present us with the improbable and the unashamedly fictive. But in their respective treatments of endings, we find that the writers are in fact grappling with the artist's problem of portraying "life as it is lived", and we find also that the solutions to the problem are different in each mode. At the same time, although Shakespeare's comedies and romances will be the main subject because they share so much in their conventions of love, sentiment, reconciliation, and the happy ending, the tragedies also deserve some brief examination. In these darker plays, the romance vision operates as an elusive alternative, beckoning towards happiness, and at least in *Antony and Cleopatra* one might detect an unexpected triumph of romance and comedy over the worldly finality of death.

Romance is an ancient and spacious mode of literature from which other, more self-contained forms have always drawn freely in the areas of conventions, narratives, character-delineation, and structural matters.[4] Tragedy, comedy, pastoral, the novel, and even to some extent lyric poetry, all find origins in the older, more inclusive, literary experience of romance. The connections are, of course, difficult to trace without forfeiting some of the vitality and originality of each particular work. The critic is liable to describe similarities so broadly that the reader may be tempted to think of all works of art being interchangeable, a matter of mere shared conventions, rather than as radically differing visions of life. On the other hand, the simple source-study may be far too narrow in its scope to awaken the sense that writers are tapping a collective source of timeless, human significance. In this essay, which is an attempt to trace the subtle interrelatedness of two recognized modes, romantic comedy, and dramatized romance, brought to perfection in the works of Shakespeare, I hope to avoid these dangers by concentrating upon one subject, the "sense of an ending".[5] In a very real sense, writers of romantic comedy and dramatized romance attempt to compress the total experience of romance into the two hours traffic of the stage: they are trying to decant a barrel into bottles. In doing so, their most tricky problem lies in ending the play in such a way that the reader or audience feels the elegance of finality, but does not lose the romance sense of potential endlessness. I shall be examining the various solutions to this problem adopted by the most proficient Elizabethan writers of romantic comedy, and in particular Shakespeare, as he develops the mode into dramatized romance. We should look first, however, in some detail at the parent, Elizabethan romance, particularly in its prose form.

At some level of our minds we seem to have the need to look forward in life and literature to an ending, either to place a boundary to pain or to reach a climax of happiness. Simultaneously, we resist finality. We want to keep going until death turns into new life, and we want happiness to go on forever. A central problem that faces writers who fashion romance stories into the dramatic mode of comedy is how to satisfy *both* emotional demands. Pure romance exists on the assumption that there will be no end, while in drama – especially Elizabethan drama – the slogan "my end is in my beginning" is insistent.

> All tragedies are finished by a death,
> All comedies are ended by a marriage,[6]

quips Byron, and death or marriage is invariably an expectation from the earliest scenes of a play. The romantic plays of Shakespeare, as we shall see, are the most profoundly exploratory and precious attempts to fuse the contradictory impulses into a simultaneous experience. He was, however, working in older fields.

A romance is potentially endless. Like the modern Western, such works as the *Morte d'Arthur*, the Palmerin cycles, *Amadis de Gaule*, and Ariosto's *Orlando Furioso* all progress in a leisurely fashion by accumulation of incidents. There is always another foe for a knight to defeat, there is always another place for him to travel to, and there is always another lady for him to fall in love with. Even after death, his sons will survive to carry on the brand in the living world, while the knight himself moves into another realm to watch the future:

> And whan that he was slayn in this manere,
> His lighte goost ful blisfully is went
> Up to the holughnesse of the eighthe spere.[7]

To ensure variety of interest, one character will disappear while the adventures of somebody else cross before our eyes, and even if the first never reappears, we trust he is still pursuing his heroic way, doing more or less the same things. "And then" is the primitive syntax that drives the romance along, reassuring us that the world will keep going, even after the book stops.

There is room, however, even in the most sprawling and accretive romances, for "the sense of an ending". They are compounds of many endings and new beginnings, series of episodes which present some immediate task for the hero, after achieving which he may move on to another. The episodes themselves lead us to expect an eventual outcome, such as the accomplishment of a major quest, the survival of an ordeal, or the winning of some special lady's hand. A quest points forward to its success or failure as unavoidably as does the beginning of a battle or a love affair, even if circumstances prevent the reader from reaching the final outcome, and even if that climax generates a new quest. There is an "ideal" romance ending projected by the mind. The central aim is survival, and the greatest quality embodied by a romance character is patience. A reason may be offered for the phenomenon that we and the characters anticipate an "ideal" ending which never quite comes. It lies in the existence of two different kinds of romance which are intimately related rather than in opposition. Romance of travel and pastoral romance are based respectively on archetypes which, when they occur together in a work, form a complete whole. Continuous movement forward through passing time marks the one, and separation of people is its strategy, while stasis and suspended time marks the other, dwelling as it does in an eternally beautiful landscape where people may find themselves and each other in peaceful harmony. Unfortunately for the characters, the former is the norm, for the pastoral is cradled as a parenthesis within the unending process of time. Examples are Shakespeare's own *As You Like It* (with its source, Lodge's *Rosalynde*) and *The Winter's Tale*, where the pastoral, although taking up much of the action, is really presented as an interlude between the active life at court, from where the characters come and back to which they must go at the end. The pastoral is in essence the perfect "ending", and yet when it ceases to lie in the future, it lies unattainably in the past. Pastoral perfection may itself be eternal, but a mortal cannot live there eternally. Book VI of *The Faerie Queene* is a beautiful but melancholy presentation of the cycle. Sir Calidore, unluckily, is defined by his courtliness, and it is his duty to live, work, and struggle in the court. He is allowed a respite from his travels and obligations in the pastoral world, although it means a temporary lapse in his knightly vigilance and his quest. Entranced by the beauty of the place and its heroine Pastorella, he would dearly love to stay. He cannot, but must return to the court, not simply as a resumption of his unending quest to defeat the Blatant Beast, but more frustratingly because he himself has caused a change in the pastoral world which has introduced jealousy, violence, and spite. This is certainly not his intention, for he is merely a carrier of the courtly diseases rather than a sufferer, and he is as dismayed as Colin Clout when his mere presence destroys the beauty, as he innocently reveals himself at the dance of the Graces. It is allowed only to poets (who, after all, are in the privileged position of having "created" the pastoral), and to wise old hermits who have renounced the court altogether, to inhabit perpetually the world of contemplation rather than action. Even between the poet and the hermit lies a distinction, for the latter must also renounce sociable pleasure and the de-

lights of love in order to win his paradise, which is both his
freedom and his limitation:

> Small was his house, and like a little cage,
> For his own turne, yet inly neate and clene,
> Deckt with greene boughes, and flowers gay beseene.
>
> (*Faerie Queene*, VI.v.38)

The poet may range more freely through time and space, and
he too has a duty. As the hermit must heal the bodies and
bruised minds of those scarred by the court, so the poet must
teach them wisdom. The pastoral world is not without its
responsibilities, although the quest involves inward ex-
ploration instead of travelling the world.

The two Elizabethan works closest to the prototype of endlessness are Spenser's *Faerie Queene* and Sidney's *New Arcadia*,
and it is no coincidence that they are unfinished. The former is
not a simple "and then" tale because, as Rosemary Freeman
says, "it is as easily systematized as a life lived",[8] and the
bottomless fertility of invention convinces us that it will go on
forever. The question "what happens next?" is complicated by
the allegorical consistency which makes us ask "why did *this*
happen after *that*?", and our answer may lie many cantos
before or many cantos after. Each book anticipates some
climax, such as the marriage of the Redcross Knight and Una,
or Guyon's destruction of the Bower of Bliss, but when
achieved, they are found to be no more than temporary res-
ting-places. The Redcross Knight cannot enjoy married bliss
for long:

> Yet swimming in that sea of blisfull ioy,
> He nought forgot, how he whilome had sworne,
> In case he could that monstrous beast destroy,
> Vnto his Faerie Queene back to retourne:
> The which he shortly did, and *Vna* left to mourne.
>
> (I.xii.41)

He reappears in the next book, when he meets Sir Guyon, just
as Sir Guyon spills over into Book III when he encounters
Britomart, and so on, while all the time Arthur is weaving his
way in and out of the action in quest of Gloriana's court. Such
an enterprise can never be fully ended, for the allegory opens

new trails in the reader's mind; but we are tempted to anticipate an ending, in the sense that we hope idealistically for
perfection in the moral and actual worlds.

The *New Arcadia* begins with a kind of ending, as two
shepherds lament the departure of their beloved Urania, and
the book is abruptly broken off in the middle of a battle. Its
structure comes to be as self-generating as that of *The Faerie
Queene*. The material seems to take over, and our expectations
of an eventual ending become increasingly subsidiary to the
multiplicity of individual experience and digressions. The
wave grows in size with the current. We follow different
characters on their independent courses, trusting to the
welfare of others, and meanwhile, leisurely digressions about
the past or about mythological characters swim in and out. At
least by Book III, Chapter 24, the wicked Cecropia has been
killed, but we feel that many more sorrows, disasters, and
reconciliations lie in front of the others before they reach the
haven of marriage, for evil is not the only adversary to virtue
and love. A character laments that Fortune is not yet aweary
of vexing her, but she strengthens herself by realizing that a
ship is not counted strong for biding one storm.[9] The cycle
moving from mishaps to ecstatic joy and back again could, as
in Spenser, go on until the end of the world.

In these two works, the Elizabethan mind draws
wholeheartedly upon the endless nature of the romance mode.
The only real equivalents in drama are the dramatic
romances, early and late. *Common Conditions* (1576) is
sustained by the pattern of separation-reunion-separation,
and the writer assumes that so long as there is an unrequited
love affair, he needs no tight dramatic structure leading up to
a climax. He can rely on the simple momentum of a narrative
to keep his audience engrossed. In order to bring the performance to an end, he allows his characters inadvertently to take
poison and die, but the liquid could just as well have been a
magic sleeping potion allowing the lovers to fight another day.
In its own words, the ending is "maruellous confusion" and
"most strange it is and pittiful beside", because the playwright
apologizes for his tedious lengthiness and abruptly stops.
Miraculous resurrections end *The Old Wive's Tale* (1590), just
as they keep the plot going in *Pericles*. These plays are different

from the romantic comedies of Lyly, Greene, and Peele, because in each the ending is not the furthest "conjectured likelihood" of an initial situation which Aristotle demands from a dramatic climax, but little more than one of several convenient places to stop. Even *King Lear*, perhaps the greatest non-comic dramatic romance, ends arbitrarily, for Lear has "died" several times already in spiritual terms, just as Gloucester comes back from what he thinks is death. The line, "Vex not his ghost. O let him pass!" (V.iii.313) could well be the self-admonition of the dramatist, who has it in his hands to stretch his characters out longer upon the rack of this tough world forever. Mercifully, he allows Lear to pass and the play to end. The question of the dramatist's manipulation of his endings will become more important in the development of this book.

Truly endless romances like the *New Arcadia* and *The Faerie Queene* are not so common in the Elizabethan age as shorter, self-contained tales, such as those by Greene, Lodge, and Rich. These short Elizabethan romances, although they carry vestiges of romance endlessness, are more artfully aware of their premeditated endings. Northrop Frye is only partially right in saying that this is an inevitable tendency as romance acquires literary pretensions:

> ... At its most naive it is an endless form in which a central character who never develops or ages goes through one adventure after another until the author himself collapses ... However, ... as soon as romance achieves a literary form, it tends to limit itself to a sequence of minor adventures leading up to a major or climacteric adventure, usually announced from the beginning, the completion of which rounds off the story.[10]

Some works bear out this generalization, but not the *Arcadia* and *Faerie Queene* which surely belong to a "literary form" and are not "naive". It is fairer to say that both kinds, long and short, are equally artful, and that the distinction lies in their imitation of different models. If medieval romance provides the structural basis, then we get Spenser, Ariosto, and the *New Arcadia*. On the other hand, if Greek romance is crossed with the Italian *novella*, then we get Sidney's *Old Arcadia* and the romances of Greene (like *Menaphon* and *Pandosto*), Lyly (*Euphues*), Lodge (*Rosalynde*), and the tales of Rich in his *Farewell to the Military Profession*. Some of these carry traces of the medieval stock by ending the story arbitrarily with a fiat from outside the action, like the intervention of a god. Others are closer to the contemporary drama, bringing about the ending from the inside, as the necessary or usual consequence of the action (in Aristotle's words), and often in the context of a judicial trial which reveals hitherto concealed evidence. The various methods of ending such self-contained romances have relevance to the development of romantic comedy. A sense of wonder predominates, and the most convenient ways of raising such an emotion are by supernatural intervention, and by recognition achieved through coincidence or through some accidental identification like a birthmark or a trinket. Behind all these methods of resolution lies an assumption about an order lying behind the action, working providentially towards the happy ending. Whether we call such providence a philosophical concept or the coercive manipulation of an artful writer is not yet important to our argument, though it will become so.

In general, supernatural intervention is not popular as a way of ending the Elizabethan romance because of Aristotle's strictures about the need for verisimilitude, but a work like Greene's *Menaphon* does use it in some sort. Just as two princes are about to be killed after being sentenced to death, there steps out from the assembly "an olde woman, attired like a Prophetesse", who explains the various mistakes that have led the men to the gallows. Only somebody endowed with supernatural powers could have this knowledge. She is linked with a realm of higher intelligences which have been watching the action from the beginning, for she points out that the predictions of an oracle, introduced in the opening pages of the story, have now been fulfilled. The gnomic oracle gives a prediction early in the story that points forward to the end, and it speaks from outside the world of tangled human relationships that make up the plot. The oracle has literary precedent in Greek works and it is used also by Sidney, but Greene's use of it is contrived and perfunctory. In Heliodorus' *Æthiopian History* and the *Arcadia*, the oracles predict but they do not intervene by proxy as in *Menaphon* to settle the business and prove themselves right. There are some short romances that end with a totally unexpected reversal that smacks of the supernatural, such as the religious miracle at the end of Lodge's *Robert the Devil*. More psychologically justifiable, but equally miraculous, is the radical change of heart by the obstreperous old father in *Forbonius and Prisceria*, when he suddenly withdraws his objections to a match between his daughter and a young man. In the latter work, there is a concept of a fortuitous providence at work. The father is swayed by his daughter's advice that he should not strive against the stream that the gods have ordained, and he admits "that it is vaine to alter that which is prefixed by destinye".[11] Crude as these endings are, they hold a significance to be picked up in comedy. There is some providential law, whether it be called destiny, the gods, or human desires, which preordains a certain ending and presides somewhere behind the action. Occasionally we catch a glimpse of a representative of such an order, like Hymen in *As You Like It*, and we sometimes have the ubiquitous presence of the supernatural order actually placed inside the action, like the gods in Lyly's plays and the fairies in *A Midsummer Night's Dream*.

To speak somewhat schematically for a moment, it might be suggested that the worlds of comedy and romance alike are governed from above by two very ancient deities emphasized by Boethius. Fortune is the fickle goddess, determined to keep the action going as long as possible by gratuitously introducing confusions and separations, just as people seem to be close to their happiness. Providence, on the other hand, is the more benevolent deity, intervening at last to solve all the problems and create a harmony which has been expected from the outset. Fortune is marginally superior, for we find romances where the ending is unhappy and even tragic, despite the fact that our expectations have anticipated joy, at least as a distant prospect. *Romeo and Juliet, Pyramus and Thisbe*, and *Othello*, for example, chart the triumph of fortune over providence, although we can in such cases make a different distinction, and say that fortune is equated with another goddess of endings, destiny. Furthermore, since the romances are unashamedly secular, we do not often find (as in Chaucer and Dante)[12] a linking of providence with the Christian God. More often, the merciful power is human love, as we see in the early play *The Rare Triumphs of Love and Fortune*, and love as a spiritual force binding people together often triumphs even when the lovers die. Whereas in the romances, such impersonal abstractions as fortune and providence are often mentioned by the narrator who assures us that they exist, in stage comedy the dramatist must build into the action itself a notion of some such controlling forces. The resolutions more often come from inside the world of the play, as the characters' love acts as the providential force. They may vehemently rail against the adversity of fortune:

> Ah cruell chance, ah lucklesse lot, to me poore wretch
>   assign'd,
> Was euer seene such contraries, by fraudulent Goddesse
>   blind,[13]

or they may thank providence for deliverance:

> And for their prouidence diuine, the Gods aboue ile praise,
> And show their works so wonderfull, vnto their laud
>   alwaies,[14]

or they may place their faith in a more humanly comprehensible force:

> O Time, thou must untangle this, not I;
> It is too hard a knot for me t'untie![15]

Behind the golden world of romantic comedy we sense a fictional order (or the hovering presence of the dramatist himself) benevolently ensuring that all will be well, but in these plays solutions must be seen to emerge from actions and feelings chosen by the characters themselves. Intrusions from the outside (whether Marcade in *Love's Labour's Lost* or Jupiter in *Cymbeline*) may be used only as a last resort, with limited control over what eventually happens. Even the miraculous resurrections of Hero in *Much Ado About Nothing* and Hermione in *The Winter's Tale* are orchestrated by human agents. Perhaps the fingers of the gods are tuning the events, but in the best Elizabethan romances and comedies we need look no futher than human love as a force of providence which may conquer fortune.

Renaissance insistence upon verisimilitude and internal consistency even in the improbabilities of the golden world makes prose fiction writers of the time suspicious of such hallowed devices as the magic potion. When Sidney uses the motif in the *Old Arcadia*, he is careful to stitch it into the narrative with elaborate explanations. By mistake, the old duke Basilius takes the potion, thought to be an aphrodisiac, but it has disastrous consequences when he falls, apparently dead. At his trial for murder, the body suddenly moves beneath its shroud, Basilius lives, and the charges must be dropped. There is no doubt the event is *like* magic to all the spectators, and the superstitious "began to fear spirits, some to look for a miracle, most to imagine they knew not what".[16] The narrator, however, will not allow the event to pass as an imposed supernatural event. Unwilling to slow down the pace of his conclusion now that marriage is in sight, he explains "in few words" but with careful attention to substantiating detail, what has happened:

> So it was that the drink he had received was neither (as Gynecia first imagined) a love potion nor (as it was after thought) a deadly poison, but a drink made by notable art, and as it was thought not without natural magic, to procure for thirty hours such a deadly sleep as should oppress all show of life . . .[17]

He even explains why the drink has first been concocted, telling briefly a romance story about Gynecia's grandmother, a princess of Cyprus, who had handed down the bottle to her daughter, without explanation.

> Which wrong interpreted by her daughter-in-law, the queen of Cyprus, was given by her to Gynecia at the time of her marriage; and the drink, finding an old body of Basilius, had kept him some hours longer in the trance than it would have done a younger.[18]

As if Sidney's artistic integrity is at stake by allowing an improbable event to have such a crucial effect on the plot, he ensures that every detail contributes to an elaborate filigree of substantiating and explanatory cross-reference, to allow the potion a ring of truth. Even the necessary pinch of romance magic is minimized by the qualifying phrase in "*as it was thought* not without natural magic". So circumstantial is the explanation that we must accept the resurrection, wonderful as it is in context, as a fully probable and necessary consequent. "Let wonder seem familiar", the Friar's words at the end of *Much Ado About Nothing*, and Hymen's speech at the end of *As You Like It*:

> Feed yourselves with questioning,
> That reason wonder may diminish,
>   (V.iv.132–3)

catch the combination of heightened mystery and rational evidence with which Sidney invests his magic potion. Almost all of Shakespeare's plays contain some such statement, bringing reason to bear upon the wonder.

Renaissance theory insists that the happy ending is most satisfactory when it does not depend on external factors. In prose romance and romantic comedy, the most common form of resolution is achieved from within the action by recognition and identification of characters through some coincidence. Amazement strikes the spectators, but the cause of the particular event is transparently clear, comprehensible without an assumption of supernatural influence. Suddenly there is a pattern where there was confusion. Often the appearance of one character is enough to make the confusions click into an orderly pattern: "Pat! He comes like the catastrophe of the old comedy".[19] It is partly the influence of stage comedy which lies behind this device in the newer, shorter Elizabethan romances, but coincidence and recognition had always been central in the most ancient romance. A public trial provides the occasion for gathering people together in *The Æthiopian History* and *Clitophon and Leucippe* and in the newer ones like the *Old Arcadia* and Greene's *Pandosto*. After the people have been assembled, all that is required is the disclosure of some vital but sometimes apparently insignificant piece of information that explains and resolves all problems. In *Pandosto*, when the old shepherd who had adopted Fawnia is condemned to die with his daughter, he feels compelled to tell the tale of how he had originally discovered the foundling when she was six days old:

Here is the chaine and the Iewels, and this *Fawnia* is the childe whome I found in the boate: what shee is, or of what parentage I knowe not, but this I am assured that shee is none of mine.[20]

The old King immediately sees the significance of the information:

Pandosto would scarce suffer him to tell out his tale, but that he enquired the time of the yeare, the manner of the boate, and other circumstances, which when he found agreeing to his court, he sodainelie leapt from his seate, and kissed *Fawnia*, wetting her tender cheeks with his teares, and crying my daughter *Fawnia*: ah sweet *Fawnia*, I am thy Father, *Fawnia*.[21]

This is enough to bring about the happy ending, the joy of which is only mildly disturbed by the heavily moralized death of the King himself.

The sparse descriptions of early romantic drama imply that recognition based on some tiny detail was the favorite method of ending plays of this kind. Stephen Gosson speaks of "the adventures of an amorous knight" who returns from his travels "so wonderfully changed, that he cannot be knowne but by some posie in his tablet, or by a broken ring, or a handkircher, or a piece of cockle shell . . .".[22] The method is a logical one for concluding works based on disguise, for the true identity will at last be recognized or revealed. Birthmarks, the favorite device for identification in the *Amadis de Gaule* cycle and other medieval romances,[23] are often used as corroborating evidence of identity in Elizabethan literature, as in *Twelfth Night*:

VIOLA: My father had a mole upon his brow.
SEBASTIAN: And so had mine.

(V.i.234–5)

The hackneyed nature of the motif is here exposed partly for purposes of parody, but even the brief glance is enough to open up the reaches of time and space of the romance world that hovers behind the courtly, golden-decadent ethos of Illyria. Rings are another form of identification which have significance, for example, in the *Merchant of Venice* and *All's Well That End's Well*. A ring allows the hero to be recognized by his father and to be married to his beloved Francelina in *The History of Palmendos*, a translation from the French by Antony Munday of part of the Spanish romance, the *Primaleon* cycle. Such coincidental identifications are further evidence of the Renaissance romance writer's desire to satisfy laws of cause-and-effect as well as evoking wonder at the sense of a power of providence lying behind the action. Perhaps it should be noted as a rider here that when Shakespeare in his last plays allows a greater degree of the supernatural, like the intervention of Jupiter in *Cymbeline*, the vision of Diana in *Pericles*, and Prospero's divine powers in *The Tempest*, he is building not upon Renaissance theory of verisimilitude but upon the precedent of the supernatural in medieval romance. In his earlier romantic comedies, which are our first concern, he may use incidents from medieval romance, but his treatment is thoroughly classical in spirit.

The feelings raised by the ending in the self-contained Elizabethan romances are summed up in the formula "joy and wonder". In many works it is no more than a formula and does not enforce much emotional assent:

> When he had a while wondered at this circumstaunce, and the truthe of euery thing laide open, and come to light, all parties were well pleased and contented.[24]

The bare bones of convention show through the skin in such examples. In other works, the writer takes trouble to raise feeling in his audience by presenting collective responses expressed by a witnessing crowd. S. L. Wolff has shown that the method of the "ensemble scene" in which a writer envisages situations "pathetically" by way of their effect upon spectators may be traced to Heliodorus, and it is used to great effect by Sidney at the end of the *Old Arcadia*.[25] Sidney allows the rapid events of the ending to play upon the stops of the crowd's feelings. But his ending is exceptional in refusing to accept the crowd's responses as final, because they would be too easy an evasion of the moral problems. The Arcadian multitude errs on the side of pity for the princes accused of murder and rape, and significantly its bias is represented by a character called Sympathus:

> While this matter was thus handling, a silent and, as it were, astonished attention possessed all the people; a kindly compassion moved the gentleman Sympathus . . .[26]

The general multitude respectfully submits to the reasoned gravity of the judge Evarchus, as he condemns the princes to death. His unsympathetic but logical judgement could have formed the ending to the *Arcadia*, thereby giving the Elizabethan audience its dose of moral doctrine. Sidney stresses the legalistic finality in the calm, impartial, and complete way in which Evarchus ("good ruler") sums up the evidence before him. Sidney even brushes aside the kind of sudden reversal that would satisfy his contemporaries. An old shepherd, Menalcas, arrives just in time to reveal the true identity of the princes and their close relationship to Evarchus, and it seems to the crowd that the revelation is enough to save the condemned men:

> Kerxenus made it known to all men what the prisoners were. To whom he cried they should salute their father, and joy in the good hap the gods had sent them; who were no less glad than all the people amazed at the strange event of all these matters.[27]

The surprised relief is arrested when Evarchus, struggling between fatherly love and a sense of duty, restates the sanctity of justice and sorrowfully refuses to alter his verdict. Law is law, whether the subject be prince or pauper. His tears move "all the assembly dolefully to record that pitiful spectacle",[28] although his sadness is not enough to prevent a feeling that he is an "obstinate-hearted man, and such a one, who being pitiless, his dominion must needs be insupportable".[29] Comparing Evarchus's conscientious behaviour to Cato's stoicism, the narrator detaches himself from the crowd's emotive response, thereby reprimanding the romance reader's desire for an easy solution. The only thing that can shake the integrity of the legal judgement is a change in the facts, and this comes when Basilius's body stirs beneath its velvet cover-

ing, "whereat every man astonished".[30] In the *Old Arcadia*,
then, Sidney uses the responses of the crowd in the final scene,
not simply as an emotional backdrop nor as a final de-
terminant of the action, but as a means of articulating a set of
collective responses that will appeal to the reader's feelings,
and as a device for playing off conventional expectations
against the true logic and morality of the situation.

Even if the "normal" collective responses at the end of
Elizabethan romances are wonder of recognition and the sub-
sequent relaxation of the marriage feast, there are frequently
tonal adjustments which remind us that life will go on after
the ending. Euphues retires to the study after his education in
the world, abandoning the feast for contemplative life. He is
stirred to "meruaile and to ioy" by the marriage of his friend,
but he himself sadly retreats from human intercourse:

> . . . Euphues gaue himselfe to solitarinesse, determining to
> soiourne in some vncouth place, vntil time might turne
> white salt into fine sugar: for surely he was both tormented
> in body and grieued in minde. . . . two friendes parted, the
> one liuing in the delightes of his newe wife, the other in
> contemplation of his olde griefes.[31]

Jacques' retreat into a monastic cave at the end of *As You Like
It* is modelled on this incident. The "happy-sad" ending,
complete with Lyly's dependence on stylistic balance and
antithesis, is carried on by his many followers in Elizabethan
romance and becomes a convention in itself. We find it, for
example, in such un-memorable works as Lodge's *Euphues
Shadow* and Austen Saker's *Narbonus, the Laberynth of Libertie*.
Acting with equanimity, and without upsetting the festivity of
the occasion, such characters extend the tonal range of the
endings with their circumspect regard for mortality. Sidney's
Old Arcadia has its sad brushstroke at the end, concerning the
author's own unrequited love, figured in "the poor hopes of
the poor Philisides in the pursuit of his affections".[32] The
"stranger" shepherd, a figure of the artist, must continue on
his solitary way, entertaining others with his melancholy
songs which spring from his own experiences. Like the
banished Kent or the old man at the end of Yeats's *Purgatory*,
he must go among new men to tell his old tales.[33] It is a

glimpse of the endlessness of the romance adventure, mirroring the endless nature of the task of interpreting human experience. It implies that any ending will only be a temporary and fragmentary ordering of emotions and that the winning of joy and wonder is a precarious and impermanent feat. The perception will mean much when we come to look at the comedies and Shakespeare's romances.

A work which makes the sad note more than a hint is also one of the most readable little romances in the period, Gascoigne's *Adventures of Master F. J.* The narrative plays off our hopes for a conventional happy ending, against the hopelessness of the lover's situation. In this book, the hero eventually recognizes the fickleness and duplicity of the noblewoman he has been pursuing. Alerted by Fraunces, who patiently loves him, F. J. overhears a conversation between his mistress and another man, which unmistakably reveals her infidelity. He demands to know the truth,

> vntil at last being still vrged with such evident tokens as he alleged, she gaue him this bone to gnawe vpon. And if I did so (quod she) what then?[34]

The brutal finality and abruptness of her reply forces him at last to abandon his suit. An embittered and sad man, F. J. immediately quits the lady's country house in which she has flirtatiously encouraged his devotions during the summer, and upon reaching a solitary place he dismounts from his horse and composes a poem, "for a fynall end of the matter". The reader has been led to recognize the obstinate fickleness of Elynor, and Gascoigne refuses to relax the tensions of the situation and to compromise the moral consistency by inserting a conventional happy ending. Even the faithful Fraunces, whom F. J. has never loved although he has used her, is left frustrated. By resisting the temptation, Gascoigne provides us with a more plausible imitation of life than is given by conventional works, even though the surprise in the ending gains its force from the expectation of the usual happy ending. *The Adventures of Master F. J.* is a minor masterpiece, its quality of writing enhanced by the emotional pressure of a thinly disguised autobiographical element, its style vigorous and economical. F. J.'s literary compositions within the narrative encourage us to see Gascoigne the artist not force-fully manipulating events, but searching for an order which is implicit in emotional experience.

These, then, are the romance elements that contribute to the characteristic ending in romantic comedy: the ancient endlessness allied to the dramatic necessity for a firm ending, the implication of some pervasive providential order, either a supernatural power or the inevitability of circumstances and instincts, and the feeling of wonder, often qualified by touches of sadness. As a bridge to considering the comedies, we should note one important difference between the romances and the plays. Because of their traditional awareness of the arbitrariness of placing an end to a story that could go on forever, the romance writers (with the exception of Sidney in the *Old Arcadia*) give a perfunctory, formulaic quality to their endings, stopping with a pithy recognition scene designed above all to enhance the element of surprise, and a glance at the "happily-ever-after" future. The plays, on the other hand, because in orthodox terms they are defined by their endings, and face the necessity to release their audiences on a high note, give a much more lingering and elaborate attention to the final scenes. Atmosphere dominates narrative, and this often forces the dramatists to make a more critical and search-ing examination of the formula which they have inherited from romance.

Romance and comedy are modes that invite, and even demand from both writer and reader, imaginative projection into a space and time that is not "here and now". Remote places are evoked, and we find ourselves in ancient Greece, the Forest of Arden or Illyria. Strange tricks are played with time. There may be a sequence of events which follows a curve of passing time, and yet there is a spell of suspended time, in which decay and death do not immediately exist. Even if death accidentally occurs, it is rarely final, for life is redeemed in resurrection or some form of new life. "Et in Arcadia ego" is an intellectual concept that occurs to the philosophical traveller in the world of romance, but it is not an immediate experience. The myth of romance appeals directly, then, to impulses that we are accustomed to regard as reprehensible in a world of pressing problems — impulses such as daydreaming, wish-fulfilment, nostalgia, indeed all forms of "escapism". Such impulses are universal, however, and if the writer's job is to describe the world as it is, including human feelings, then part of his job is done in presenting and justifying such states of mind which may, indeed, be less idle and escapist than they are regarded.

Spenser, in his "Mutabilitie Cantos", provides the most elaborate defense of the romance attitude to time, pointing out that change is cyclical, and has its place within a permanent order of existence:

> For, all that moueth, doth in *Change* delight:
> But thence-forth all shall rest eternally
> With Him that is the God of Sabbaoth hight.[35]

Much of what I have said implies that the poet often regards himself as the god presiding over his own world of the imagination, a clairvoyant seer into the truth of a permanence which can be attained in art. It is significant that in Spenser's debate between mutability and eternity, the poets are given a prominent place, and that the occasion is likened to a wedding,

> Where *Phoebus* self, that god of Poets hight,
> They say did sing the spousall hymne full cleere,
> That all the gods were rauisht with delight
> Of his celestiall song, and Musicks wondrous might.[36]

For the poet, the marriage ceremony is the meeting place of short time and eternity, the social celebration of an event which signifies the wished-for culmination of every love affair, holding at bay the forces of decay and death. Here, in the significance of a moment, we come close to the inner meaning of the endeavors of writers of romance in its many different modes. They attempt to fuse comedy and tragedy, endlessness and the sense of an ending.

II The sense of an ending in early Elizabethan romantic comedy

The romantic comedies of Lyly, Greene, and the young Shakespeare did not quite spring like lightning out of a clear sky though, as F. P. Wilson points out, their antecedents are not immediately apparent:

> But what of romantic comedy? Where are the anticipations before Lyly and Greene and the young Shakespeare of the comedy based upon the love between the sexes, the settled mode of the great age of Elizabethan comedy? It is extraordinary how few traces have survived.[1]

The plays in fact come fairly clearly through a direct path from contemporary prose romance and other romance sources, but we cannot track the development very closely into the drama, for most of the dramatic romances which appear to have been so popular during the 1570s and '80s have been lost.[2] The fact that they are lost may ironically be largely due to their very popularity, since they do not obey the lofty, Aristotelian criteria for literary works codified, for example, in Sidney's *Defence of Poetry*. It is a pity we cannot know more about such plays because the fact that they eventually led to Shakespeare's own late plays gives them a teasing significance. It would not be the last time that a hierarchy of critical "authority" has written out of the canons of literary history works which are rather more attractive to the ordinary folk who were beginning to go to the theatre than to the academic purists or polemicists. (One might compare the unsuccessful attempts by Dryden, and by Leavis and Eliot, to obliterate all traces of Milton.) Despite our lack of evidence about the interim plays, we can say that Elizabethan romantic comedy achieved a rapid maturity because it learned many lessons from the already well-developed mode of narrative romance. The stage was to take over wholesale many plots, conventions, attitudes, and deeper visions from romance as it was known at the time: "*A Palace of pleasure*, the *Golden Asse*, the *Æthiopian historie*, *Amadis of Fraunce*, the *Rounde table*, *baudie Comedies* in *Latine*, *French*, *Italian*, and *Spanish*, have beene thoroughly ransackt to furnish the Playe houses in London".[3] The main problem facing the dramatists who wished to adapt romantic stories into plays was how to foreshorten a multitude of incidents into a compact form. One solution adopted was to single out love as the pre-eminently central subject. In romantic comedies we are led from early in the play to anticipate a liaison based on love between at least one woman and one man at the end. No matter how surprisingly our expectations are granted or thwarted, at least the direction is clear. In this way the dramatist can subdue all digressive interests by hanging firmly onto a simple center, relegating other potential diversions by creating a polyphonic use of "sub plots", orbiting around a set of primary relationships. The other solution gradually developed and explored by the writers of romantic comedy was to fashion a particular kind of open-ended conclusion, which can accommodate the conflicting impulses at work in the romance narrative.

Pre-Shakespearean romantic comedy

In the plays of John Lyly, the eventual outcome is usually arranged by gods who have greater powers than the mortals whose destiny they direct. G. K. Hunter says that in the "debate" structure of Lyly's plays, various points of view are kept in "a state of permanent unbalance keeping the action in movement", until balance is restored "by some fiat from outside".[4] "Outside" is the wrong word. Lyly's gods are as much "within" the action as his mortal characters, just as Titania and Oberon are as "real" in the play-world as Duke Theseus. They are characterized in the same fashion as the humans, with similar temperamental differences and weaknesses, and they are often implicated just as deeply in the problems as the other characters. The difference is that they have special powers and superior knowledge. Perhaps Lyly discovered this technique from early plays on the model of *The Rare Triumphs of Love and Fortune* where the goddesses, Venus and Fortune, quarrel about their respective powers, test their cases by observing a love affair between two mortals, and eventually intervene to manufacture jointly a happy ending for the mortals, who are "amazed quite, confounded euery way".[5] The goddesses display human susceptibilities to jealousy, anger, and gloating triumph. In Lyly's plays, too, romance clichés about Love and Fortune are presented concretely in particularized characters.

In *Love's Metamorphosis*,[6] Cupid and Ceres are the ruling deities who attempt to bring about a marriage between three lovesick young men and three hardhearted women. The play is full of delicate ironies. While Cupid can change the women into objects, he cannot change their minds without help from Ceres, and even after her intervention, the women's capitulation is heavily qualified and conditional, introducing an amusingly realistic attitude towards romantic love. After being re-metamorphosed into human shape from a stone, a rose, and a bird, the women, far from feeling humiliated and grateful, demand that the recalcitrant elements in their personalities, such as flintiness, prickliness, and flightiness, be acknowledged and accepted by the men before they will marry. Similar concessions in the other plays point to the limitations on the divine beings in their control over the independent human mind. Cynthia in *Endimion*, although she has the power to send Endimion into an endless sleep and turn Bagoa into a tree, cannot prevent the yearning adoration shown to herself by Endimion. She is forced to accept it, without having any desire or power to return it. She cannot persuade or compel the mortal man to fall in love with a convenient human woman. Human love, and emotions in general, are forces beyond the control even of the immortals. In *Gallathea*, the supernatural society has distinct limitations and sanctions placed upon its powers, and each character is subject to human feelings. The god Neptune is thwarted of the annual tribute of the fairest virgin in the land. Venus, unable to persuade two mortal women out of their love for each other, is driven to the extreme of turning one of them into a man so that love may be requited. The love itself is irrefutable. Cupid, after attacking Diana's nymphs, is punished by Diana. Cupid is characterized as a mischievous boy, using his power irresponsibly:

> . . . *Cupid* though he be a child, is no babie. I will make
> their paines my pastimes . . . Whilst I trewant from my
> mother, I will vse some tyranny in these woods . . .[7]

We grow accustomed to the stubborn irascibility of Neptune,
to Venus's impatience, and to Diana's wary, uncompromising, but gracious spirit, and the ending represents a hard-won
compromise between these three powerful gods, paralleling
the qualified harmony restored to the mortal world. Lyly's
endings are not necessarily imposed, facile, or arbitrary, because the characters who untangle the knots, despite the
existence of supernatural powers, must solve their own problems, come to terms with each other, and consistently be true
to themselves. Balance and harmony between Cupid and
Ceres, Cynthia and Dipsas, Venus and Diana, are achieved at
a psychological level and are not externally manipulated.

In their tone, Lyly's endings are far from the exhilarating
release of saturnalia, the freeing from responsibility felt in the
social ritual of a holiday which the work of C. L. Barber has
encouraged us to see as the norm of Elizabethan romantic
comedy.[8] Instead, Lyly is the master of the heavily qualified
ending. The debates that his plays present are not susceptible
to easy black and white solutions, and he does not shirk
compromise as the most convincing and illuminating resolution. His characters must concede as much as they win,
making allowances for the irrationality and intransigence of
the human mind under the effect of love. *Gallathea* ends with a
rocking antithesis between Diana's injunction that the lovers
must accept that their affections cannot be consummated
because "nature will haue it so, necessitie must", and Venus's
faith in a higher power of instinct: "What is to Loue or the
Mistrisse of Loue vnpossible?"[9] The final outcome is left
hanging, for we never know which woman is to be changed
into a man. A specific poignancy is evoked by the sense of a
painful compromise between the golden world of fictions and
the brazen world of reality, with few illusions about the precarious nature of the solutions adopted to love problems in
either. Contrived and artificial as his plays are in language
and structure, Lyly, with tactful *mimesis*, builds into his endings the suggestion that endings do not necessarily conclude.

As we shall come to see, it is his plays rather than such pieces as *Summer's Last Will and Testament*[10] which provide Shakespeare with his prototype for the comic ending.

Robert Greene's mature comedies, on the other hand, end in a far more robustly conclusive manner. Admittedly, he does point into the future, but with such secure optimism that we feel happiness has been established as a permanent state, and there is no room for further complications. Just as at the end of Shakespeare's *The Two Gentlemen of Verona*, universal joy creates the generous spirit of forgiveness. At the end of *James the Fourth*, the King of England magnanimously forgives the erring James, expresses optimistic patriotism and faith in a love that ensures the future of his line and his kingdom:

> Thou provident [kind] mother of increase,
> Thou must prevail, ah nature, thou must rule.[11]

The presence of the entire body of the English and Scottish armies, taciturn "good men at arms", broadens the domestic, marital reconciliation into a national affair, emphasizing the restoration of unity to the land. Similarly, at the end of *Friar Bacon and Friar Bungay*, the magician stands

> . . . joyful that this royal marriage
> Portends such bliss unto this matchless realm.[12]

He uses his magic to prophesy the glorious future of England.

The success of courtship in Greene's plays depends upon the strong-willed patience of his heroines and their faithful adherence to a belief in love. At the end of *Friar Bacon*, Margaret, the pastoral maid, having chosen the nunnery after Lacy has apparently abandoned her, is suddenly given the choice of marrying:

ERMSBY: Choose you, fair damsel; yet the choice is yours,
    Either a solemn nunnery or the court;
    God or Lord Lacy. Which contents you best,
    To be a nun, or else Lord Lacy's wife?
LACY: A good motion. Peggy, your answer must be short.

MARGARET: The flesh is frail. My lord doth know it well,
That when he comes with his enchanting face,
Whatso'er betide, I cannot say him nay;
Off goes the habit of a maiden's heart,
And, seeing Fortune will, fair Framingham,
And all the show of holy nuns, farewell. ·
Lacy for me, if he will be my lord.[13]

Her yielding tone and easy rhythms contrast with the peremptory, abruptly jovial demands of the courtiers, and her acknowledgement that "the flesh is frail" cuts through their dishonest cruelty. The ending is more solidly based upon a single virtue, patience, which will continue into the future, than upon the subtle, precarious balances that create equilibrium at the end of Lyly's plays. In order that the loose ends be tied up, there must be a double marriage at court:

LACY: Peggy, thy lord, thy love, thy husband
Trust me, by truth of knighthood, that the king
Stays for to marry matchless Eleanor
Until I bring thee richly to the court,
That one day may both marry her and thee.[14]

In a vision of national unity, the gentle, pastoral world is wedded to the court.

All Greene's romantic comedies, like the vast majority of Elizabethan romances and most of Shakespeare's comedies, end with a thumping invitation to a feast. As in *Henry V*, the final marital happiness and national optimisim are clinched and celebrated with food and wine:

Come, royall father, enter we my tent:—
And, soldiers, feast it, frolick it, like friends:—[15]

There is no scepticism about the fragility and artifice of the romance ending, no shadow of death nor qualms about the future. Greene's endings are wholly festive, depending on a virtue firmly within its own world, faithful constancy. They are "endless" only in the realm of the fairy or folk tale's "ever-afterness". His endings are more specifically "comic" than Lyly's, and although Shakespeare inevitably takes something of Greene's tones, he tends very early in his career towards the more problematic and equivocal qualities that he could find in Lyly's conclusions.

Shakespeare's first steps

Shakespeare was nothing if not an astonishingly fast learner. His originality can often be seen not so much as innovation, but as blending in a new and unique way materials that lay close to his hands. This is certainly true of his first two attempts in comedy. In *The Comedy of Errors* he takes a completely classical source and sews onto its ending the form of romance reconciliation, sentiment, and conclusiveness that he could find in Greene's plays. He accomplishes the feat with a perfect grace, and the stitches do not show. In *The Two Gentlemen of Verona* he uses material more conventionally associated with romance, and ambitiously attempts to emulate Lyly in providing a morally qualified ending. This time, artful and neat as the overall design may be, he cannot be said to match the genius of Lyly in this one respect. The relative failure of the ending to convince us is of importance, since it leads Shakespeare on to the new experiments in other plays, and it signals also a kind of self-knowledge in the dramatist which is to surface later in the "problem" plays, a recognition that he cannot fully achieve the romance ending without overt manipulation of his story, and without forfeiting a measure of the internal variety, verisimilitude, and complexity which he has given his characters.

Although *The Comedy of Errors* is built upon a classical play, the ending owes more to romance than to the hard-edged satire of Plautus's *Menaechmi*.[16] It is full of wonder, emotional reconciliation of a family, and a sense of the improbable (although, in good Aristotelian fashion, the dénouement is a "probable and necessary" consequence of a series of events: Shakespeare is as careful, and as classical, as Sidney.) In many ways, the ending is similar to that in Heliodorus's ancient prose romance, the *Æthiopian History*. The "ensemble"[17] witnessing the events includes, amongst attendants and many other officers, a duke who acts as a stage "audience" voicing the general feelings when identities are revealed. He is a detached and puzzled spectator: "stay, stand apart; I know not which is which". Both as adjudicator and emotive watcher, the Duke interprets the occasion for us. In his judicial capacity, he intervenes directly to effect the happy ending by removing the shadow of death from Aegeon, and he then merges with the crowd as one who "will gossip at this feast". He is a spokesman for the crowd in its various attitudes, questioning, wondering, explaining. Sons are restored to their father and the Abbess turns out to be the long-lost mother. Despite the Duke's suspicion that they have all "drunk of Circe's cup" (V.i.270) and the repeated insistence that they must all be living in a "dream", there is no magic or supernatural knowledge required by anyone to untie the knot. It is done by a coincidental concurrence of events. The characters "accidentally are met together" and the mysteries are solved. There are no loose ends, no threats from outside the world of the play — only the "nativity" of a family which is akin to a rebirth for individuals. The last lines emphasize the finality of an ending implicit in the very beginning:

> We came into the world like brother and brother,
> And now let's go hand in hand, not one before another.
>
> > [*Exeunt*

Shakespeare softened the harsh edges of his Roman source with various changes, additions, and developments, some of which relate to romance. Geoffrey Bullough, in his monumental work on Shakespeare, points out by changing the location from Epidamnum to Ephesus, the dramatist gives himself three new possibilities.[18] First, since it is the place where St. Paul stayed for two years, we find some stern Pauline doctrine about domestic unity, a subject which culminates in the reconciliation of the family by the end of the play. Secondly, in Bullough's words, "Ephesus was a place of sorcerers and exorcists, and 'curious arts' as St. Paul states",[19] and Shakespeare exploits this memory both explicitly (I.ii.97 ff.) and in the deployment of the fable itself, which shows characters who think they must be under the influence of "Dark-working sorcerers that change the mind" as they encounter such weird confusions. Thirdly, Ephesus was classically important for its Temple of Diana. Bullough here gives only half the significance:

> Does the Ephesian locale explain why the Mother becomes an Abbess, in reminiscence of the Temple of Diana with its priestesses?[20]

The other half of the explanation lies in the fact that Diana herself has a special place in romance, and it is this detail which proves that Shakespeare was consciously "romancing" the ending of his comedy. We remember from our reading of *Pericles*, perhaps the purest romance that Shakespeare wrote, that Diana actually appears in that play in anticipation of the ending which also involves the reconciliation of a family. *Pericles* was to be solidly based on the story of Apollonius of Tyre, and it too is a story of shipwreck, love, separation, and reunions. In the recognition scene where the Abbess is presented in *The Comedy of Errors,* Shakespeare is drawing upon romance conventions in general, and the Apollonius story in particular. He had, then, encountered the territory long before he wrote *Pericles*, in a most unlikely context of reshaping the Latin comedy. Already he has begun to draw upon the genre which was to become his most familiar haunt.

The Two Gentlemen of Verona turns wholly to romance for its story and its spirit. It is built upon love, travel, and male friendship, and it gives us Shakespeare's first disguised heroine. The main source is Montemayor's *Diana Enamorada*, wedded slightly uneasily with the tradition of the duties of friendship exemplified by *Euphues*, and more fluently with other romances such as the ubiquitous *Arcadia*.[21] We find a lyricism and emphasis upon sentiment totally absent from *The Comedy of Errors*. We find also a development of the use of the servant figures deriving from the hapless Dromios, for Launce and Speed serve as ironically distorting mirrors for their masters when the latter fall in love.[22] Although the mesh between the "serious" love affairs and the ridiculous may not be altogether smooth and tight, yet it is easy to see in the device the origins of Shakespeare's self-critical vision in which romance is never allowed to go unchallenged by a more abrasive and unromantic point of view. When he is to employ romance, its motifs are presented with a self-consciousness which toughens the alluring and lyrical sentiment, while softening the antiromantic attitudes by constant appeals to sincere and strong feeling.

The ending of *The Two Gentlemen of Verona* depends on the formula of recognition, but it requires the further exercise of forgiveness to close the story satisfactorily. In very general terms, romance and romantic comedy reward the good for their patience in adversity, and allow for the defeat of the bad. A spirit of generosity expresses itself, as R. G. Hunter argues in *Shakespeare and the Comedy of Forgiveness*,[23] when erring characters are forgiven and allowed to go unpunished. Greene's comedies are illustrations, although the forgiveness is sometimes too easily won. Margaret forgives Lacy far too readily for the modern mind to endorse. Lyly's concern to restore equilibrium to his comic world by moral compromise is a symptom of the spirit of forgiveness, and perhaps more convincing than Greene's volte-faces. *The Two Gentlemen of Verona* ends with the gracious gesture of allowing the characters — and the audience — to forgive Proteus. But if we compare the source with the play, we find a huge and glaring difference. The account in Montemayor (translated in later years by Yonge) is full of the spirit of genuine forgiveness from the wronged woman, and her feelings are explained by her deep love:

> The Shepherdesse, *Felismena*, who saw *Don Felix* so penitent for his passed misdeeds, and so affectionately returned to his first thoughts, with many teares told him, that she did pardon him, because the love, that she had ever borne him, would suffer her to do no lesse: which if she had not thought to do, she would never have taken so great paines and so many wearie journeyes to seeke him out, and many other things, wherewith *Don Felix* was confirmed in his former love.[24]

Extraordinarily, in *The Two Gentlemen*, Julia is never even asked whether she forgives Proteus, for the main issue is the forgiveness by his friend Valentine for betraying him, and Julia's words are, if anything, very bitter and accusatory:

> Behold her that gave aim to all thy oaths,
> And entertain'd 'em deeply in her heart.
> How oft hast thou with perjury cleft the root!
> O Proteus, let this habit make thee blush!
> Be thou asham'd that I have took upon me
> Such an immodest raiment — if shame live
> In a disguise of love.
> It is the lesser blot, modesty finds,
> Women to change their shapes than men their minds.
>   (V.iv.101–9)

Rather than fully confessing his guilt, Proteus merely reflects that Julia is just as beautiful as Silvia, and pronounces condescendingly that he has his "wish for ever". Julia's curt "And I mine" is our only evidence that she is content. Shakespeare has, then, consciously abandoned the totally generous feelings given to him by his source, and in the process he has hit a note which may be called sceptically censorious, realistic, or structurally unsatisfactory, depending on whether our primary interest be ethical, psychological, or aesthetic. Already, and in this apparently insignificant comedy, Shakespeare is anticipating a scepticism about the validity of fictions which becomes more comprehensively worrying in *Measure for Measure* and *All's Well That Ends Well*. Where the ethics of love are involved (rather than simple recognition as in *The Comedy of Errors*), it seems that Shakespeare's moral integrity compels him towards an inconclusive or consciously "flawed" ending.

There seems to be a deliberate attempt to mute or confuse the moral problems raised by the situation, which makes it misleading to speak of forgiveness as the be-all-and-end-all of the climax in this play. In his behavior towards Sylvia and Julia in the final scene, Proteus reveals himself as a would-be rapist, totally fickle and faithless (but then, "In love, Who respects friend?" (V.iv.53)). Valentine's first reaction is one of outraged moral condemnation:

> Thou common friend, that's without faith or love —
> For such is a friend now; treacherous man,
> Thou hast beguil'd my hopes . . .
>
> (V.iv.64–4)

He swears never to trust the man again, and at this point his impulses seem healthily angry, even considering the wayward affability of Proteus. None the less, as soon as Proteus recognizes his sins and repents —

> My shame and guilt confounds me.
> Forgive me, Valentine. —
>
> (V.iv.73–4)

then Valentine replies not with *hauteur*, nor with grudging acceptance of the apology, but with an extravagant and excessive gesture of forgiveness:

> And, that my love may appear plain and free,
> All that was mine in Sylvia I give thee.
>
>   (V.iv.82–3)

A different code of behaviour must suddenly be understood. The jingling couplet betrays the fact that Valentine is giving a programmed answer, consciously striving to conform to a conventional code of male friendship.[25] His gesture is dangerously close to the manifestly absurd action of the wandering knight, Eumenides in *The Old Wives' Tale*, when he agrees to cut his woman in half to order to reward Jack, the ghost who saved him:

> EUMENIDES: Well ere I will falsifie my worde unto my friend, take her all, heere *Jack* ile giue her thee.
> IACKE: Nay neither more nor lesse Maister, but even just halfe.
> EUMENIDES: Before I will falsifie my faith unto my friend, I will divide hir, *Jacke* thou shalt have halfe.[26]

The Old Wives' Tale is written throughout in this burlesque vein, but Valentine's magnanimous gesture comes hard on the heels of his more credible response which confuses the issue. When the penitent Proteus admits the shame of inconstancy as Julia reveals her identity, there is some conviction behind his blank verse, but then once more a jingling rhyme signals the conventional sentiment and posture:

> Inconstancy falls off ere it begins.
> What is in Sylvia's face but I must spy
> More fresh in Julia's with a constant eye?
>
>   (V.iv.113–5)

Like Valentine, Proteus is referring his conduct to a conventional standard, this time constancy. The human feelings voiced in spontaneous resentment by both Valentine and Julia become confused again. How do we interpret this? Virulent feeling would be out of place in a thorough parody, but simple-minded conventionalism would be unworthy of the sincere feelings occasionally voiced in the play. Perhaps by overlapping different moral standards — impulsive, conventional, and violently strained — Shakespeare is making a point about the well-meaning muddle of the young men.

Or perhaps it is more convincing to say that the ending to this play brings Shakespeare up against a fundamental problem involved in writing the kind of dramatized romance that Lyly writes, the problem of how to draw together both a resistance to glib, romance formulae, and a corresponding consistency to the moral problems raised by the action of the play. His answer in this play is to sacrifice consistency of morality to the jovial tone. Proteus's callousness to women is treated as venial in the good-natured happiness of the marriage feast:

> Come, Proteus, 'tis your penance but to hear,
> The story of your loves discovered.
> That done, our day of marriage shall be yours;
> One feast, one house, one mutual happiness!
>
> (V.iv.170–3)

Like many readers (though perhaps not audiences in the theatre), I find the ending to *The Two Gentlemen of Verona* unsatisfactory in an interesting way. The ending is theatrically effective, but at the expense of moral consistency. As if recognizing that in this play he has not matched Lyly's subtlety of resolution, Shakespeare never again simplifies his endings by falling back so facilely on a handy formula, or relying upon the audience's desire for a fully comic ending.

He does not, however, give up the attempt to create the comic ending which will also be complex enough to gather into itself an adequately comprehensive recognition of the vitality, changeability, and moral qualities of the characters who people his plays. In fact, Shakespeare worries away for the rest of his writing career at the problem of how to adapt into his dramatic endings the potential endlessness of romance. In his mature romantic comedies, from *Love's Labour's Lost* to *Twelfth Night*, he succeeds in working fully within the world of romance conventions, while expanding the significance of these conventions to accommodate some of the rougher facts of a life outside the play. The plays to follow stand as monuments to the notion culled from romance of reconciliation and betrothal as a resting-place that may be temporal, but yet one that partakes of the endless and eternal. The most impermanent and fragile of moments is invested with a precious significance of timelessness. Shakespeare leads us in each play through a struggle which allows such a moment to come, and he gives us enough brief hints to make us aware that it will surely pass into the archives of memory as quickly as time itself. He does not deny that "all that moueth, doth in *Change* delight", but by the end of each play we are aware that change, and the vicissitudes of past and future are given a meaning by the joy of the consummated present. Each play is *sui generis*, but they all share at the end the mixed emotions of wonder in timelessness, and regret at the fact of passing time. In the formal terms of literary history, Shakespeare, building upon the experiments of Lyly and Greene, perfects such a delicate experience by finding ways of fusing together the "endlessness" of romance and the necessity for an ending imposed by the medium of drama. Even in his two earliest comedies we can find the seeds which will blossom so wonderfully in his maturity.

III Shakespeare's mature romantic comedies

Love's Labour's Lost is another attempt by Shakespeare to write the kind of romantic comedy pioneered by Lyly, where the ending is qualified and open. The stroke he uses to solve the problems inherent in the form is daringly simple, for he simply denies the credibility of the conventional happy ending, almost gratuitously going out of his way to provide a complicating factor. The direction of our expectations in the play is clear and conventional. The action seems to be moving towards a declaration of marriage. From the opening there is little doubt that the sterile vow of celibacy will crumble before the shattering power of love, and this is what happens. The pageant of the Nine Worthies seems calculated to relax the mood into the festivity of betrothal. Little resistance poses itself to the courtships, since the ladies' coyness is, we find from their conversations, a teasing test of the men rather than a denial of their suits. The vitality lies not in true conflict, nor in any complexity of debate about love but in the fertility of language, the women's shrewdness, and the energetic release of the men when they fall in love. However, as if it is too easy for the dramatist to satisfy our expectations, and as if love should not be won so easily by men who have denied its existence, resistance is introduced in the form of a chilly message from the outside world:

> *Enter a messenger*: MONSIEUR MARCADÉ.
> MARCADE: God save you, madam!
> PRINCESS: Welcome, Marcade;
> But that thou interruptest our merriment.
> MARCADE: I am sorry, madam; for the news I bring
> Is heavy in my tongue. The King your father —
> PRINCESS: Dead, for my life!
> MARCADE: Even so; my tale is told.
>   (V.ii.703–9)

This strikes a grim note, intruding from a more distressing and succinctly spoken world into the charm, chatter, and hyperbole of the King's curious knotted garden.[1] The King tries to sustain the spirit of gallant courtship, but he is quite rougly rebuffed:

KING: Yet since love's argument was first on foot,
Let not the cloud of sorrow justle it
From what it purpos'd . . .
QUEEN: I understand you not; my griefs are double.

(V.ii.736–40)

Even after sober declarations of love from the men, the ladies are still not able to treat the proposals except as "pleasant jest and courtesy, As bombast and as lining to the time." In Lyly's fashion, a compromise is struck. The ladies will mourn for a year in France, the men are to undergo certain taxing experiences such as living in a hermitage or a hospital to learn genuine self-denial and understanding of people's problems. After the educative process the courtship may (or may not) begin afresh.

The play ends with chastened self-awareness on the part of the men and reluctant withdrawal on that of the women:

BEROWNE:
Our wooing doth not end like an old play:
Jack hath not Jill. These ladies' courtesy
Might well have made our sport a comedy.
KING:
Come, sir, it wants a twelvemonth an' a day
And then 'twill end.
BEROWNE:
That's too long for a play.

(V.ii.862–6)

Berowne's rueful comment is more than just a statement about form, since it points towards a moral lesson which the men ought to have learned during the action. They have throughout treated life as a play and other people as merely objects for their own amusement. After the vow to study has been taken, Berowne asks, "But is there no quick recreation granted?" (I.i.159), and the King replies that Armado the Spaniard will serve their turn:

> But I protest I love to hear him lie,
> And I will use him for my minstrelsy.
>
> (I.i.173–4)

Longaville agrees, adding another human toy to their re-
pertory:

> Costard the swain and he shall be our sport;
> And so to study three years is but short.
>
> (I.i.177–8)

The low-born characters are eventually used mercilessly for
the "sport" of the courtly, when their humbly offered entertainment of a masque is mocked off the stage in derisive
laughter and in a manner which is "not generous, not gentle,
not humble" (V.ii.621). To emphasize the point, after this
touching line from Holofernes, the shadows lengthen on the
world of play: "A light for Monsieur Judas! It grows dark, he
may stumble" (V.ii.622). The courtiers have played loose
with their oaths, have attempted to play with the lives of the
women, have condescendingly played with the low-born
characters, and they have played with language, turning every
word inside out for a joke. Of course, such things are
appropriate to a stage comedy, but a life may not be res-
ponsibly led on such a basis. "That's too long for a play" uses
the word in at least two senses. By drawing attention to the
play as artifice, Shakespéare reminds the audience that it too
is about to leave the playful world for one more serious. The
hints pointing to the necessity of leaving the golden world for
the brazen gather as the end comes in sight. Armado sees his
duty for the future through the little hole of discretion, and
swears marriage to Jaquenetta, and she too is directed into the
future for she is "quick, the child brags in her belly already".[2]

When the action "doth not end like an old play", it is
tempting to see the separation as Shakespeare's rejection of
the conventions of literature itself, as if from this point
onwards he is not writing a work of art but somehow showing
us "life" directly. It is worth remembering, however, that he
could in fact find many prototypes for such an ending in
romance. Apart from Gascoigne's *The Adventures of Master F. J.*
and Lyly's *Euphues*, which give us saddened retreats, there are

more clear-cut analogues. In Malory's *Le Morte d'Arthur*, Sir Marhaus, Sir Gawain, and Sir Uweyn make an oath to separate from their chosen damsels and to return "that day twelve monthe". "And so they kissed and departed."[3] (Gawain's lady is lost and the other two, at the end of the twelve months, effect a permanent separation, which shows that we cannot be so sure of happiness in the world of romance as in comedy.) At the end of *The Parliament of Fowls*, the female eagle, wooed by three males, asks Nature to allow her to postpone her choice for a year. She advises the lusty suitors:

> Beth of good herte, and serveth alle thre.
> A yer is nat so longe to endure.[4]

Book I of *The Faerie Queene* ends with the Redcross Knight leaving his newlywed Una in order to pursue his quest of the Blatant Beast, "The which he shortly did, and Una left to mourne."[5] Certainly Shakespeare in *Love's Labour's Lost* is exhibiting a general wariness about the authenticity and validity of fictions, yet he is, ironically, also drawing on a fictional model in doing so. Romance includes in its vision many separations and reunions, and it is often arbitrary which of the two events will be chosen to end the work. Comedy, on the other hand, characteristically closes with happy harmony. With the arrival of Marcade, a messenger whose forebears lie in Greek tragedy, Shakespeare stops writing comedy and begins to write romance. It seems a paradox in the light of the unashamed fictiveness of this genre, but he is also representing something more "realistic" than we find in a comedy where Jack hath Jill and all will be well.

The little songs sung by the Worthies after the action, a timely lightening of the tone, continue the disengagement from the play's golden world. Nothing could be further from the pontifical words of the King at the beginning when declaring the plan for the academe. Instead of lofty abstractions like fame, death, time, honor, and eternity, the songs modestly depict rapid vignettes of real life: the sight of flowers and the sounds of birds in spring, physical hardship in winter, evidenced by cold hands, frozen milk, and red noses, with their homely, cosy compensations like the prospect of roasted crab apples sizzling in a pot of ale while greasy Joan keels the pot. The songs accept, without any attempt at evaluation, the contradictions in the seasons: delight and sexual uncertainty in the spring, adversity and warmth in the winter. The repeated syntax, "When . . . then . . ." suggests the underlying idea that everything is "fit in his place and time" (I.i.98).[6] A new attitude towards time's open-endedness, and a new mode of expression (a ballad statement by an uncourtly, rustic voice outside the play world, rather than the dramatic utterance of a character in context) takes us further outside the self-contained fictional world of the play about protected university-types. The direction is appropriate to the overall ideas presented by the play, for the men have discovered that the cloistered attempt to discover truth is barren and offending against the law of nature, because, if they had listened, they would have known that "it is the simplicity of man to hearken after the flesh". They must accept the brazen uncertainties of the future before committing themselves to the world-without-end bargain of marriage.

Love's Labour's Lost is Shakespeare's first successful attempt to square up the moral problems raised by the narrative with the necessity for an ending. It is also his first considered attempt to fuse the comic expectation of an ending with the romance tendency towards endlessness. Inconclusive as it is, the play-world is brought to an end with a regretful explanation that the future is too long for a play. The final comment, whatever its authorial sanction, is teasing. "You that way; we this way" is perhaps the final separation of the play world (where the characters either go back into their fictional world and visit hospitals, or they take off their play clothes and become people like us) and our own world, as we leave the theatre and walk home, or close the book and prepare supper. Since our own minds must still be partially engaged with the fate of the courtiers, speculating upon whether they will marry or not at the end of the year, endlessness rolls before the worlds of fiction and of fact, despite the attainment of a temporary resting place in both, the end of the play.

After showing a delicate mastery of the Lylian presentation of romance, ending with a careful compromise that balances and sets against each other the conflicting tensions raised in the action, Shakespeare could conceivably have gone on to remain within such a dramatic world. Instead, he chooses to take a slightly different course. In *A Midsummer Night's Dream* he partly repeats the experience, but he extends radically an element which is present in *Love's Labour's Lost* but not emphatically. In the *Dream* we are faced with a curious sense that the play is functioning fully within the conventional assumptions of romance, and yet also contemplating itself, in a self-conscious way, inviting us to explore the boundaries between romance and the reality outside what we may loosely call the world of art. The play achieves such a double perspective by centering around the metaphor of the dream, and by making the ending of the play highly elusive and shifting. Here we have a new dimension added to the "endless ending". Convinced by the illusion, we may remain within the world of the artifice; and yet simultaneously we are encouraged to disengage ourselves from the action, and contemplate it from a more rational distance. With this play, Shakespeare develops a critique of romance expectations, as he did in *Love's Labour's Lost*, but not yet so drastic a questioning as to imply that he is losing faith in the potency and utility of fictions. A more radical challenge is to be posed in later plays.

The elusiveness of *A Midsummer Night's Dream* as a whole can be appreciated when we simply try to locate where the actual ending of the play lies, as a point in the action. Aristotle would have some trouble specifying the point "which is naturally after something itself, either as its necessary or usual consequence, and with nothing after it."[7] Does the resolution lie in the awakening of Titania, the awakening of the lovers, the rout of Peter Quince's play, or the fairies' benediction pronounced upon the marriage house? In this play, which has so many wonderfully overlapping qualities, it is possible to see the inherent tendency of romantic comedy to give a vision of endlessness sustained in one long ending. In his first three scenes, Shakespeare characteristically presents three little societies one by one — the court, the artisans, and the fairies — and although unexpected twists will occur, there is never much doubt where each is leading. The need to draw the strings together becomes a matter of urgency as early as III.ii:

> My fairy lord, this must be done with haste,
> For night's swift dragons cut the clouds full fast.
>
> (III.ii.378–9)

At the very end the dramatist shows some solicitude for the audience, as he gently allows each society the courtesy of its own farewell, as if acknowledging that we are reluctant to leave his fictional world:

> And farewell, friends;
> Thus Thisby ends;
> Adieu, adieu, adieu.
> . . .
> Lovers, to bed; 'tis almost fairy time
> . . .
> Trip away; make no stay;
> Meet me all by break of day.
> . . .
> So good night unto you all.
> Give me your hands, if we be friends,
> And Robin shall restore amends.
>
> (V.i.335–427 *passim*)

The ripples of farewells move outwards until they wash around the audience. Having seen what, at the time, the audience thought would be the last performance of Peter Brook's production of the play, I can testify to the strange sense of exhilaration, nostalgia, and reluctance to leave, inspired in the audience by this rocking, endless ending.

The atmosphere of the play is created largely by the sustained use of the dream metaphor, and the ending is marked by the repeated idea of awakening. Hippolyta's compressed prediction at the beginning sets the direction:

> Four days will quickly steep themselves in night;
> Four nights will quickly dream away the time.
>
> (I.i.7–8)

So quickly does this happen that the four nights are telescoped into one, and the events packed into that night are "swift as a shadow, short as any dream" (I.i.144). There is even a trace of the medieval dream vision of the *Roman de la Rose*. The lovers,

after entering the woods contemplating those doctrines of love
that they "could ever read, Could ever hear by tale of history",
are confronted with situations which bring fictional
statements to life in such an explicit way that we are reminded
of Chaucer falling asleep over "the Dreem of Scipioun" and
dreaming of the parliament of fowls. The ending is made up of
a series of awakenings. First is that of the fairy queen:

> OBERON: Now, my Titania; wake you, my sweet queen.
> TITANIA: My Oberon! What visions have I seen!
> (IV.i.72–3)

The wonder of romance is conveyed in the awakening of the
four lovers. "Half sleep, half waking" (IV.i.146) they tell
Theseus that overnight their feelings have changed, and they
cannot tell how or why. They are not sure whether they are in
the land of the waking or the dreaming:

> DEMETRIUS: These things seem small and undistinguish-
> able,
> Like far-off mountains turned into clouds.
> HERMIA: Methinks I see these things with parted eye,
> When everything seems double.
> (IV.i.184–7)

It is impossible to be sure grammatically what the repeated
"these things" refers to (the events of the night? the lovers'
present condition? Theseus's retinue?), and in the lovers'
dazed state of bewilderment, it is unfair to enquire too closely.
The experiences of the night and the present happenings of
the morning seem unreal, the one displaced and distorted by
the perspective of the other. Gradually the lovers mark the
limits of what they think to be dream and reality by mentally
"pinching themselves", checking and synchronizing the respective versions of the latest fact, the arrival of the Duke.
Demetrius concludes:

> Why, then, we are awake; let's follow him;
> And by the way let us recount our dreams.
> (IV.i.195–6)

They are left not only with hazy recollections of a strange,
dream-like ordeal, but with some proof of its occurrence,

Dementrius's new-found love for Helena. This identifiable vestige of an intangible experience further confuses the boundary between being awake and being asleep. It should be stressed, however, that the lovers have not been dreaming. We have watched their doings when they were under the sway of fairy power, and we must accept the truth of the events, even if we want to interpret it more as a figurative than literal truth, showing the volatile, dream-like caprice of young love.

Bottom likens his time with the fairy queen in the woods to "a dream past the wit of man to say what dream it was" (IV.i.204), but in his inimitable way he extends the experience to the status of "a most rare vision". His is no idle, deceptive dream, but a vision full of religious significance, as his confusion of I Corinthians, 2:9 shows:

> The eye of man hath not heard, the ear of man hath not seen, man's hand is not able to taste, his tongue to conceive, nor, his heart to report, what my dream was!
>
> (IV.i.208–11)

The biblical version ends not with "my dream" but with "the things which God hath prepared for them that love him." Bottom's wondering, respectful awe shows that he accepts the episode as a God-given insight into truth. In many ways, his choice of allusion is appropriate in the context of romance. In the biblical version, Paul is justifying faith in the Spirit as a mystery, contrasted with things accessible to mortal reason which he describes as "the wisdom of man", and which he subordinates to faith. In echoing this doctrine, Bottom unwittingly casts light on the action of *A Midsummer Night's Dream* and on the spirit in which we should approach literary romance. "The wisdom of man" as voiced by Theseus can make nothing of the strange happenings in the forest, and he sees them as "antique fables" and "fairy toys" told by infatuated lovers who are as deranged as poets and madmen:

> . . . the natural man receiveth not the things of the Spirit of God: for they are foolishness unto him: neither can he know them, because they are spiritually discerned.
>
> (I Cor. 2:14)

We, who have witnessed the deeds of Oberon and Puck, have more faith in the mystery. But even for us, there remains the impenetrable and talismanic secret of the magic flowers. The humble love-in-idleness, simultaneously the secret of love and the speckled pansy, challenges us to dismiss it as a "weak and idle theme", dares us to be so childish as to believe in its magical properties. And yet love is such a sub-rational affair that we dismiss the flower at our peril. Irrational, improbable and artificial as the events of romance may be, the mode is capable of carrying a "great constancy" apprehensible by those willing to awaken their faith. At the same time, *A Midsummer Night's Dream* is a "self-conscious" romance, since the contrary view, Theseus's voice of reason, finds its place alongside the mysterious motifs of true romance. The ending gives us a "goodnight" from both Theseus and Puck.

The interlude, "Pyramus and Thisbe", another story from romance, serves the double function of relaxing the tone into that of a happy wedding feast, and it creates yet another recession into a fictional world. "It is nothing, nothing in the world" (V.i.78) protests Philostrate, and indeed the play is "like a tangled chain; nothing impaired, but all disordered" (V.i.124). For that matter, though, the whole of Shakespeare's play is "nothing" in its elusive insubstantiality. The interlude has all the old romance features: "A lover that kills himself most gallant for love" (I.ii.19), a lion (which appears in the *Arcadia* and *Rosalynde*), and a lady loved by the hero, moonlight (paralleled in the *Arcadia*, Montemayor's *Diana*, Sannazzaro's *Arcadia*, and many other romances), but it has nothing so incredible as fairies or the transformation of a man into an ass. The artistic effect that Peter Quince aims at is close to what the *Dream* as a whole achieves:

> Gentles, perchance you wonder at this show;
> But wonder on, till truth make all things plain.
>
> (V.i.126–7)

The ending, though hinging upon remorseless death instead of Ovid's metamorphosis of the lovers into the dark red berry of the mulberry tree, retrieves something for the future. Pyramus's soul is in the sky, and in good *Romeo and Juliet* fashion, "the wall is down that parted their fathers" (V.i.342).

The differences between "Pyramus and Thisbe" and the *Dream* as a whole lie not in the materials, but in the respective attitudes to artifice. Ignoring such aspects as plausibility of conduct, consistency of atmosphere, truth of human responses, and so on, Quince concentrates on matters which Shakespeare leaves to our "imaginary forces," like bringing the moonlight onto the stage. The artisans make the same mistake as Frolick in *The Old Wives' Tale* when, hearing about the "King or a lord, or a Duke that had a fair daughter", he worries about "Who drest his dinner then?"[8] They show unawareness of art as an illusion capable of creating a self-sufficient and convincing world which "grows to something of great constancy, But howsoever strange and admirable" (V.i.26–7). Like Theseus, they ignore the call to faith and imagination necessitated by the romance mode, hinted at by Bottom and St Paul. Perhaps this is why Theseus enjoys the play, whereas the imaginative Hippolyta is irritated by it.

The courtiers' ridicule of the players is directed mainly at the literal-mindedness of the mechanicals' attempts to create verisimilitude, but they do not realize a quiet irony at their own expense. The play of "Pyramus and Thisbe", seen as a romance whose dénouement depends on chance, accident, and an unseen force of "Fate", resembles the events which the lovers have themselves encountered in the woods. When Hermia extends to Helena her wish that "good luck grant thee thy Demetrius" (I.i.221), she speaks prophetically: it *is* good luck, no more, no less. In romance the actual result, death or marriage, is sometimes arbitrary, and these lovers are fortunate that the deities placed in temporary control over their destiny (and the permanent deity, the dramatist) are benevolent, while the "Fates" ruling the lives of Pyramus and Thisbe are less sympathetic. The lovers have no right to criticize the genre of dramatic romance, and if they had the distance and insight of a Feste each would admit that "I was one, sir, in this interlude".[9] Even Theseus cannot complain of the seething brains and shaping fantasies of poets, for without them he would never have existed. Such thoughts are whimsical but, as well as illustrating Shakespeare's apparent lifelong obsession with the sin of ingratitude, they seem to be invited by the play itself. Its series of overlapping endings folds the play inwards in a series of receding artifices, until we wonder whether the life which the play relinquishes us to is yet another vision, "No more yielding but a dream".

The Merchant of Venice gives a different compromise between the comic ending and the romance desire for endlessness. It is again debatable what we call the ending, for there are two distinct dramatic climaxes, each followed by quieter, anti-climactic sections. The first climax is the scene in which Bassanio chooses the leaden casket and plights his troth to Portia (III.ii). The scene is ceremonial and hushed, full of rapt expressiveness of love and joy:

> O love, be moderate, allay thy ecstasy,
> In measure rain thy joy, scant this excess!
> I feel too much thy blessing. Make it less,
> For fear I surfeit.
>
> (III.ii.111–4)

Bassanio likens his confusion to the effect in a crowd of a prince's speech,

> Where every something, being blent together,
> Turns to a wild of nothing, save of joy
> Express'd and not express'd.
>
> (III.ii.182–4)

Nerissa happily cries "Good joy, my lord and lady", and she immediately wins a husband in Gratiano. They begin to discuss the feast which will celebrate the two marriages, and they even joke about who will have the first child. If the prime issue were the marriage of Portia, the play is more or less over at this point, and there are all the trappings, the "wonder" of the comic ending in the treatment of the scene. The rest of the play is about married love rather than courtship, and even in this context, the course of true love does not run smooth.

The action continues with the news of Antonio's financial ruin. From here on, we build towards the second climax, the confrontation of Portia and Shylock in the courtroom (IV.i). The development might be interpreted in different ways. As many critics have noted,[10] the play presents a running debate about value, measured by feelings or by finance. Even Portia is described in monetary terms as the golden fleece, "nothing undervalu'd To Cato's daughter, Brutus' Portia" (I.i.165–6), and many Jasons come in quest of her. Even Bassanio comes as a fortune hunter. This makes the marriage less crucial than the resolution of the clash between conceptions of value based on money, epitomized most starkly in the actions of Shylock, and conceptions of value based on love and friendship, belonging to Portia in Belmont. Alternatively, we could place Portia herself even closer to the center, and say that the play shows her developing in character from weary fatalism generated by the mercenary aims of her suitors and the lax, aristocratic boredom of one who cannot "choose" her destiny ("so is the will of a living daughter curb'd by the will of a dead father" (I.ii.18–22)), to the point where, after the "lott'ry" has been settled, she takes her own future into her own hands. With adaptable independence, she takes on the barrister's role and dominates proceedings. It is she also who brings news to Antonio of the successes of his argosies, and as if she has herself become now a representative of powers of providence, she will not disclose " by what strange accident" she chanced on the letter. (More cynically, however, we might suspect that she has paid the bill herself from her massive wealth.) No matter what overall structure we choose to find in the play, it is a peculiar comedy in that it keeps going long after the celebration of marriage. Like the romances, it presents a vision of cycles moving from joy to disaster to joy, into the future.

The play keeps going even after the triumph in the courtroom. Act Five, so easily seen as a flat anticlimax after the tenseness of the struggle against Shylock, seems designed to retrieve the ethic of love after the severe challenge made to it, but even so, there are odd tonalities. The lyrical aria between Lorenzo and Jessica as they sit upon the bank, watching the moonlight and recalling mythical lovers, strikes a note of idealism, but it thickens in a kind of cloying self-indulgence as the music plays. The poetry seems to mark time to the point of stagnation, with a waiting expectancy, and 110 lines pass while all that happens is the setting of the moon. Normally, the tempo of a romance or comedy quickens after the climax, but here it moves with a deliberate slowness. There is even a touch of disease in the air. "This night methinks is but the daylight sick." (V.i.124) Suddenly, however, as Portia is reunited with Bassanio, a cascade of puns on "light" switches the play into a bantering tone that lasts until the end. Unfortunately, even this climax cannot be seen unequivocally as the joyful festivity of reconciliation, for the jokes hide barbs. The two pairs of lovers have their first quarrel when they discuss "the rings", and even though we are confident that the women are simply playing a game, there seems to be an element of self-righteous power domination in the way they keep the men on edge for so long. Is this Shakespeare's sardonic prediction of the future of their marriages, in their bickering over trivia? For the women, there is an important point at stake, for they are seeking to establish the principle of fidelity in relationships. They indignantly harp on the "false heart" that will give away a betrothal ring, as if its value is no more than mercenary: "I'll die for't but some woman had the ring." (V.i.208) There plays about the rings themselves an ambiguity, for they are regarded by the men as mere trinkets, by the women as profoundly significant symbols. Bassanio with shamefaced exasperation splutters that they have given to the lawyers the rings given by Portia and Nerissa:

> Sweet Portia,
> If you did know to whom I gave the ring,
> If you did know for whom I gave the ring,
> And would conceive for what I gave the ring,
> And how unwillingly I left the ring,
> When nought would be accepted but the ring,
> You would abate the strength of your displeasure.
>
> (V.i.192–8)

The interchange demonstrates anything but an easy, affectionate exercise of romantic forgiveness, considering that the ring is an ancient motif of recognition from romance. In this play of "struggle",[11] even reconciliation between lovers has its distresses. In this case the women, when they admit that they were the lawyers, use the rings to inform the men that they have all shared in the arduous and frightening trial in the courtroom, emphasizing the mutuality of suffering in love. The loss of the rings also threatens momentarily the happiness of the two couples, and to this extent the women use the episode to symbolize the trust and fidelity necessary to the shared quality of love. By shaming the men, they also establish some dominance in the relationships. At the same time, Bassanio's refrain "the ring" brings laughter to a theatre audience, and the laughter sounds a challenge to a convention in which tiny trinkets may somehow embody experiences and relationships. *Othello* takes the hint past harmless parody. The loss of a handkerchief, an even more mundane object, has disastrous consequences, because of the symbolical value accorded it by one character who pins his faith on the romantic vision of life. In the comic world, the potentially tragic chain of events is arrested by a timely disclosure, and a return to common sense, but there is a lurking suspicion that the happy state may not be permanent.

If *The Merchant of Venice* gives us an ending distinguished by its capacity to "keep going" into and through incipient disaster, it also excludes one character from the *bonhomie* of festivity. Shylock is the clearest example of what Northrop Frye calls the "scapegoat" figure, upon whose distress the comedy is secured. Compassionate actors and critics have seen Shylock's fate as too harsh for a comedy, but in the moral stresses of the play it is defensible. Shakespeare, by the very direction of his comedy, has played advocate on behalf of love and forgiveness, though he has tested them both thoroughly, and he has placed himself against a devil who respects only the "compulsion" of the law without recognizing any concept of mercy:

> My deeds upon my head! I crave the law,
> The penalty and forfeit of my bond.
>
> (IV.i.201–2)

The brazen world of legality and money is directly challenging the ethics of the golden world of feelings. The integrity of the writer forces him to provide a genuine resolution, like Sidney in the *Old Arcadia*, without evading the terms of the struggle. Portia must attack and defeat Shylock with legalistic arguments, for he respects no others. The Jew has placed himself outside a society based on human values, and he resists all appeals to sympathy and forgiveness:

> By my soul I swear
> There is no power in the tongue of man
> To alter me.
>
> (IV.i.235–7)

His implacable ruthlessness is condemned even by the judge, who feels that at law he must uphold the Jew's claim. Having defeated Shylock with his own form of reasoning, logic-chopping, and mercenary legalism, it is not only just but imperative that Portia, on behalf of the forces of love, must extract the full penalty. In fact, Antonio extends to Shylock the "mercy" of allowing him to live, and giving him the use of half his goods during his lifetime. The deeper irony, of course, is that the defendants themselves are not entirely innocent of Shylock's offenses. Portia's suitors have been mercenary, including Bassanio, and Antonio makes his living as a speculative merchant. The crowing rudeness of Gratiano in the courtroom is considerably less than generous. And Shylock himself has explained that his tactics are valid in a world where Jews are few and Christians are many:

> O father Abram, what these Christians are,
> Whose own hard dealings teaches them suspect
> The thoughts of others!
>
> (I.iii.155–7)

The tenuous answer is that whereas Shylock is consistently mercenary and revengeful, the Christians are redeemable because of their basic ethics of human value. Bassanio, for all his faults, does learn from the milieu of Belmont, and chooses the leaden casket, instead of consistently seeing human worth in terms of monetary worth. Because of their implication in the Jew's guilt, however, the Christians cannot afford to be complacent. They should see his defeat as an event which exorcises an element in their own society. Shakespeare is trying to establish a principle or concept which is not represented wholly in any one character, and it is the absence of an embodiment of this principle which forces the dramatist to test with vigilance every action and assumption. As a consequence, Antonio is left alone at the end, a minor scapegoat. Because his trade is money, he is given a monetary reward for his generosity, but he must endure the loneliness of a man who does not base his life *fully* on an ethic of love. The ending of the play must "keep going" because the basic threats to its world are still at large, just as the Blatant Beast is at large after Book VI of *The Faerie Queene*, and more aptly, as Mammon is untouched by his encounter with Sir Guyon.

After the three previous comedies which present variations on the "endless ending", *As You Like It* returns to a straightforward celebratory ending in the fashion of Robert Greene and *Henry the Fifth*. Even the play's closely followed source, Lodge's *Rosalynde*, is not so weightily concluded as the play. The dramatist slows down the tempo of the last action, expanding what was a rushed and relieved summary in the prose work into a slow, ceremonial occasion, noticeable after the chatty conversationalism and pace of the rest. The two or three pages at the end of *Rosalynde*, where the interest shifts from love to the national welfare as the Duke triumphantly leads his men back to overthrow the tyrant, are eliminated in the play and replaced by a miraculous conversion of the bad Duke when he enters the skirts of the forest. Even he is brought into the fold, and poses no future threat. There are some anticipations of trouble. Jaques bequeaths to Touchstone "wrangling; for thy loving voyage Is but for two months victuall'd" (V.iv.185), recalling for a moment Rosalind's advice that maids are May when they woo, but the sky changes when they are wives. Jaques himself, remembering Euphues, serenely leaves the wedding feast for sober contemplation. His retreat is the "tremor in the balance" described by Anne Barton, but it is not allowed to cause us distress.[12] Nothing really threatens the moment of "true delights," and the aesthetic finality is as marked as the emotional:

> First, in this forest let us do these ends
> That here were well begun and well begot.
>   (V.iv.164–5)

Shakespeare even pulls the trick of introducing a new character, Hymen, to establish the mystical nature of the marriages.

He has no need of this supernatural introduction. In Lodge's work, the capable resourcefulness of "the amorous Girle-boy"[13] holds the situation in firm control after she reaches the forest, and she carefully prepares and effects the *coup de théâtre* in which all she need do is display her true identity to bring about the happy ending. No supernatural influence is needed. Earlier in the story, the disguised Rosalynde comforts her lover by saying that she has a friend "that is deeply experienst in Negromancy and Magicke, what art can do shall be acted for thine aduantage",[14] but this is simply a reassuring fiction without significance for the plot. Shakespeare is taking up Lodge's hint of magic, and he makes the ending *seem* like a spell. Rosalind decides the time has come to draw the couples to the ark in marriage, after Celia and Oliver have vowed their love. Orlando is showing impatience with the charade, and needs more tangible reassurance:

> ROSALIND: Why, then, to-morrow I cannot serve your turn
>   for Rosalind?
> ORLANDO: I can live no longer by thinking.
> ROSALIND: I will weary you, then, no longer with idle
>   talking . . .
>
> (V.ii.46–8)

This is a curiously intense moment, for both recognize – Orlando with irritation, Rosalind with disappointed pique – that they are no longer playing games of words and disguises, but playing in earnest with their future lives. With businesslike briskness, Ganimede promises to bring together Rosalind and Orlando, Phebe and Silvius, on the morrow when Celia and Oliver are to be married. The claim is that magical power is involved:

> Believe then, if you please, that I can do strange things. I have, since I was three year old, convers'd with a magician, most profound in his art and yet not damnable.
>
> (V.ii.57–60)

The claim is emphasized by repetition:

> ORLANDO: Speak'st thou in sober meanings?
> ROSALIND: By my life, I do; which I tender dearly, though I
>   say I am a magician.
>
> (V.ii.64–6)

Although sceptical, Orlando is inclined to believe the story:

> I sometimes do believe and sometimes not.

> But, my good lord, this boy is forest-born,
> And hath been tutor'd in the rudiments
> Of many desperate studies by his uncle,
> Whom he reports to be a great magician,
> Obscured in the circle of this forest.
>
> (V.iv.3 and V.iv.30–4)

The repeated emphasis on the supposed magical powers of Ganimede establishes a sense of romance mystery, even if we detect a Puckish joke by Shakespeare that it is he, as dramatist, who is Rosalind's tutor, who can bring about whatever ending he wishes. The several sets of phrases that suddenly break out, take on the force of incantations, as if all the characters are spellbound: "And so am I for . . ."; "I will marry/satisfy/content you . . . to-morrow"; "You say that you'll . . ."; "Keep you your word . . ." (V.ii.75–101). Rosalind breaks the spell, for it is too early: "Pray you, no more of this; 'Tis like the howling of Irish wolves against the moon" (V.ii.103–4). But the spell-like tone is re-established in the final scene. The formality with which Rosalind and Celia are presented in their own persons by Hymen, a divine figure mysteriously produced and accompanied by "still music", takes us into yet another mode, reminiscent not so much of the magic spell as the neoplatonic axioms of marriage as an earthly analogue of divine harmony:

> Then is there mirth in heaven,
> When earthly things made even
> Atone together.
>
> (V.iv.102–4)

After the heightened, ceremonial song of Hymen in praise of marriage, there is hushed economy in the interchange, as Rosalind is recognized, and reconciled with her father and lover. The patterned, rocking repetitions are noticeable after the flexible speech rhythms of the dialogue before this final scene:

ROSALIND: [*To Duke*] To you I give myself, for I am yours.

[*To Orlando*] To you I give myself, for I am yours.
DUKE SENIOR: If there be truth in sight, you are my
 daughter.
ORLANDO: If there be truth in sight, you are my Rosalind.
PHEBE: If sight and shape be true,
 Why then my love adieu!
ROSALIND: I'll have no father, if you be not he;
 I'll have no husband, if you be not he;
 Nor ne'er wed woman, if you be not she.

          (V.iv.110–18)

Only Phebe's plaintive wail (the shift in tone indicated by the
different meter), hints that the identity of "Ganimede",
understood by the audience throughout, is now clear also to
the characters. The masque-like stasis of the wooing tableau is
broken on the entrance of Jaques de Boys, to report the
situation outside the woods, and an air of busy activity is
resumed with rustic revelry.

Unlike Viola at the end of *Twelfth Night*, Rosalind retires,
takes off her disguise, and returns before the betrothals.
Whereas in the prose account, the narrator can simply tell us
this, and bring her back without more ado, the dramatist must
fill a vacuum while Rosalind changes, and attention falls on
the chatter of Touchstone. When she returns, the tone has
altered. She is now a limited character, Rosalind the court-
dweller, and no longer the forest-born magician. This is one
reason why Hymen takes over the role of controlling deity,
imposing upon the woman a limited place in the human
pattern of betrothals after her period of freedom in disguise. In
fact, she does not say a word after the wedding song sung by
Hymen, until the epilogue. The case reverses that of Viola.
Rosalind has been liberated by her masculine disguise, able to
speak her mind and exuberantly act out her impulses, and
when she takes off the disguise there is inevitably a narrowing
of the range of emotions and activities expected from her.
Rosalind is literally brought down to earth, and the exercise of
destiny which she has held in the forest must now be yielded
up to a more coercive form of providence, social conventions,
as represented in the conservatism of the comic ending.

The figure of Hymen may have been suggested to Shakespeare by Lyly's gods, but the dramatic function is different. Hymen does not adjudicate but presides; the character does not influence the plot but indicates the existence of a mystical hierarchy above the human courtship. The marriage is in this case no compromise but an inevitable outcome of expectation. Hymen does not belong to any characterized society like the fairies in the *Dream* and the gods in Lyly. The best comparison for the scene, I think, is Spenser's *Epithalamion*. Both are intended as offerings to the socially sanctioned deity of married love, in order to elevate the occasion above individual common experience:

> And thou great Iuno, which with awful might
> The lawes of wedlock still dost patronize,
> And the religion of the faith first plight
> With sacred rites hast taught to solemnize:
> And eeke for comfort often called art
> Of women in their smart,
> Eternally bind thou this louely band,
> And all thy blessings vnto vs impart.
>
> . . .
> And thou fayre Hebe, and thou Hymen free,
> Grant that it may so be.
> Til which we cease your further prayse to sing,
> Ne any woods shal answer, nor your Echo ring.[15]

Spenser's poem, of course, is written throughout in this reverential, unhurried way, whereas Shakespeare has to make a radical shift of tone in order to achieve such a plateau in this play. He creates in a new way the sense of endlessness demanded by romance by lifting the events of the betrothal from the temporal flux into the realm of stable social harmony. The pains of courtship, its bullying, its strategical, testing lies (signalled by Rosalind's disguise), its moments of animal rapacity, and its sharp distresses, are all gathered into a moment when the *significance* of the event is celebrated. For a short time, the ending of *As You Like It* is an endless monument to the capacity of betrothal to clarify, surpass, and consummate a period of time by establishing a form of stability.

Rosalind's epilogue snatches back for a moment the

abrasiveness of prose after the ceremoniousness of poetry, as a reminder of what has led up to the betrothals. She speaks now not as a representative of fortune, nor in the figure of Ganimede who had been liberated by disguise to speak about women from the outside. She speaks for the dramatist who has been playing games of invention upon us: "My way is to conjure you". As if to emphasize the mischievous element of feigning throughout the play, Rosalind suddenly speaks as a boy-actor: "If I were a woman . . ." "If" is the language of hypothesis, summing up the conjectured likelihoods of the golden world which are pressed upon us by the conjuring of the dramatist.[16] By making us now aware of the strategy he has been employing, Shakespeare takes us a step away from the magical delights of the marriage scene and from the jubilant pastime in the forest of Arden, and allows us to slip back into the world without close.

In *Much Ado About Nothing* Shakespeare presents yet another variation on the comic/romance ending. The nature of the experiment might be summed up by saying that he manages to fuse two different kinds of material which are potentially discrepant, and he does so by giving equal attention to two sets of relationships. The "love" between Claudio and Hero comes from the world of romance, although in essence the presentation threatens our belief in romantic sentiment. The love between Beatrice and Benedick mingles aspects of the rough and tumble English comic tradition (*Gammer Gurton's Needle* and *The Taming of a Shrew*, supplemented by Shakespeare's own *The Shrew*) with something we might call a more realistic social observation. Paradoxically, just as the romance plot comes to challenge romance itself, so the "realistic" plot represents a far more solid and trustworthy basis for romantic love between man and woman. The paradoxes emerge partly out of the blend itself, for we are encouraged to compare and contrast the behavior and feelings of the two sets of lovers. The ending introduces new complexities.

Partly it is the strong definition of a total society in Messina which allows Shakespeare to encapsulate the two kinds of material in a single focus. In this little society, with its constant gossiping, eavesdropping, "noting", and suspicion,[17] no relationship goes unnoticed. Such prying vigilance eventually exposes weaknesses in the literary, romantic ethic of love based on appearances, while fostering a strong-minded wariness about the precariousness of relationships in the mature, open-eyed lovers. But eventually the tides merge with each other at least for one moment in the flow of "wonder" which marks the prototypical romance ending, followed by the ebb of circumstantial explanation to be delivered after the play is over:

> FRIAR: All this amazement can I qualify,
> When, after that the holy rites are ended,
> I'll tell you of fair Hero's death.
> Meantime let wonder seem familiar,
> And to the chapel let us presently.
>
> (V.iv.67–71)

The formula hardly varies from play to play, although the tone of the ending is profoundly different. In this play, for example, we should not underestimate the effect of the social ethos, created partly even by the purely comic characters, Dogberry and his little group of Keystone cops. They, the official "watchers", prefer to sleep while the other characters are scrutinizing each other closely, and yet they inadvertently reveal a truth which nobody else sees. They mangle words while their courtly betters are speaking so elegantly and wittily, and yet they are able to communicate in far more honest and straightforward terms than others are capable of.

The Hero-Claudio plot has almost purely romance sources, ranging from the ancient Greek erotic romance, *Chaereas and Callirhoe*, to the sixteenth century *Orlando Furioso* by Ariosto, and stories by Bandello, together with contemporary Italian plays.[18] It is identified by the most time-honored conventions of romance such as love at first sight, the bed trick, the false death, and the apparent resurrection. We find the characteristic blend of tones (expressed in poetic rhetoric whereas the rest is in prose), ranging from the language of sentimental love to the somber dirge, artificial in expression but full of tragic feeling:

> Pardon, goddess of the night,
> Those that slew thy virgin knight;
> For the which, with songs of woe,
> Round about her tomb they go.
>   Midnight, assist our moan;
>   Help us to sigh and groan,
>   Heavily, heavily.
> Graves, yawn, and yield your dead,
> Till death be uttered,
>   Heavily, heavily.
>
> (V.iii.12–21)

We would expect such a chivalric, romantic plot to be full of the generous, optimistic, and amorous vision which we associate with the mode. But by this time Shakespeare is beginning more than just to hint at a retreat from romance conviction, and there is much to make us suspicious. Claudio is a soldier, and conducts his love affair somewhat like one, plotting, campaigning, and eventually bullying his lover. He loses faith in her fidelity almost instantaneously on the basis of a rumor without even bothering to investigate, and refusing to believe in her chastity. His language at this point is rejective and self-centred:

> But fare thee well, most foul, most fair!
>   Farewell,
> Thou pure impiety and impious purity!
> For thee I'll lock up all the gates of love,
> And on my eyelids shall conjecture hang,
> To turn all beauty into thoughts of harm,
> And never shall it more be gracious.
>
> (IV.i.102–7)

Something has gone very sour when romance sentiment can so rapidly become untrusting and ungenerous, and we begin to glimpse the origins of a Troilus and an Othello, both so romantic in their affection, so vituperative in their mistrust of female sexuality. Even the ending does not retrieve the purity of wonder, because Claudio seems ready again to fall in love with the appearance of Hero, without really showing that he has learned much about himself or about the woman. "Which is the lady I must seize upon" (V.iv.53) and "Why, then she's mine" (V.iv.55) are hardly reassuring statements in their content, and far from wondering in tone.

Beatrice and Benedick, presumably older and more experienced, appear to have abandoned romantic expectations. Each advises the younger person of the same sex against commitment to love:

CLAUDIO: Can the world buy such a jewel?
BENEDICK: Yea, and a case to put it into. But speak you this with a sad brow, or do you play the flouting Jack to tell us Cupid is a good hare-finder, and Vulcan a rare carpenter? Come, in what key shall a man take you to go in the song?
CLAUDIO: In mine eye she is the sweetest lady that ever I look'd on.
BENEDICK: I can see yet without spectacles, and I can see no such matter.

(I.i.155–62)

Benedick's mockery of conventions from romance literature is matched by Beatrice's debunking tone when she advises the younger woman:

For, hear me, Hero: wooing, wedding, and repenting, is as a Scotch jig, a measure, and a cinquepace; the first suit is hot and hasty, like a Scotch jig, and full as fantastical; the wedding, mannerly modest, as a measure, full of state and ancientry; and then comes repentance, and, with his bad legs, falls into the cinquepace faster and faster, till he sink into his grave.

(II.i.60–7)

We rapidly gather, however, that these two are using the tone of superior worldy-wisdom to conceal (even from themselves) their own feelings, and by dwelling upon their mutual determination *not* to marry, they reveal ironically to all around that they are preoccupied with each other with a strength of subliminal feeling that must culminate in marriage. This is precisely what happens, after Don Pedro and his accomplices plot to pull down the defenses of wit and wariness so cleverly built up by the characters themselves. There is a clear parallel in the way that one brother, the taciturn Don John, destroys a relationship through subterfuge, while Don Pedro, through equal manipulativeness, "creates" a love-affair, as if they represent respectively the malignant and benign operations of a single social strategy which controls and determines personal relationships. Indeed, one might even see them as personifications of Fortune and Providence in the romance world. Another mark of the society is a strict segregation of the men and the women into different camps, and communication between the two must be conducted at a distance, either through conventions, through aggressive wit, or sometimes through deviously coded messages (employed most subtly between Beatrice and Don Pedro). The destructive potential in such a state of sexual apartheid is unleashed over the affair of Hero's alleged unchastity, and the men and the women retreat into belligerent positions of separate loyalties. The situation is of great importance to Beatrice and Benedick since their new-found access to a mutual and direct communication is at stake. It should already be clear that the play is neither affirming nor challenging romance conventions alone. It is a play about social conventions themselves, in which courtly manners and literary conceptions of love are included but are not the totality. Under such complex conditions, the ending of the comedy cannot possibly be a simple one.

In attempting to break the deadlock between men and women that exists after the broken marriage, Beatrice proposes something which challenges romance conventions and the comic ending. She asks Benedick to cross the picket lines and join the women, and she does so in a chilling manner. When she requires him to prove his love for her and to "Kill Claudio!" (IV.i.287), she is laying down a condition which will ensure her own future confidence in Benedick, but she is also threatening the fabric of the comic ending. It is a challenge to the playwright to recognize his options, a potential invitation to be consistent to the moral vision of a play which has presented Claudio as reprehensibly untrusting, untrustworthy, and undeserving of the woman's love. The moment had come in *Love's Labour's Lost* and almost in *The Two Gentlemen of Verona*, and again it is not allowed to destroy the comic vitality. We are presented with a much safer and more comfortable resolution with the "resurrection" of Hero from her grave. But just for an instance we are dared to contemplate directly the potential dishonesty involved in manipulating the comic ending, the element of arbitrariness involved, all in the context of a play which throws a somewhat sardonic light on the manipulative, coercive tendencies of society itself. However, as the chasm yawns, it is equally quickly covered over by the timely willingness of Benedick to assist in the comic compromise, and all is well. By a hair's breadth, romance wins its battle against social realism. The moment hardly exists outside the time it takes to say the lines, for it stands so far from the providential benevolence of the romance fictions which create the plot and which lead us to expect a happy ending. The momentary tremor, however, does rapidly open a vein which we will find running through *Twelfth Night*, a suspicion that the comic, romance world is fragile, impermanent, and vulnerable.

Much Ado, a play full of wonderfully functional parallels and contrasts in the structure, turns upon an unexpectedly archetypal distinction between night and day, for as the malevolent deeds are done by darkness, the benevolent ones are done under the sun-ripened honeysuckle. The point of change, marking the delicate balance, comes at a significant moment after the "burial" of Hero:

> DON PEDRO: Good morrow, masters; put your torches out;
> The wolves have prey'd; and look, the gentle day,
> Before the wheels of Phoebus, round about
> Dapples the drowsy east with spots of grey.
>
> (V.ii.24–7)

In *Twelfth Night*, Shakespeare returns to the formula for ending *The Comedy of Errors*, coincidence. No one character has the special knowledge needed to end the confusions, and it must be left to the whirligig of time to bring its own revenges. All that is needed is the physical proximity of the twins, and it is simply a matter of time before this happens. The wonder of recognition in the romance world fills the spectators, who at first "throw a strange regard" (V.i.204) upon Sebastian and Viola. Duke Orsino exclaims in amazement:

> One face, one voice, one habit, and two persons!
> A natural perspective, that is and is not.

(V.i.208–9)

Olivia's response is "Most wonderful" (V.i.217). As the truth dawns, there is the feeling of awakening from a dream, for each character is at one and the same time an outsider and a participant, seeing double, as through a "natural perspective".

The source for *Twelfth Night*, Rich's short, Italianate romance, "Of Apolonius and Silla", does not climax with such eloquent simplicity. The Viola-figure tears off her clothes to the waist and reveals her sex – a gesture which might happen in a prose work but hardly on the stage. The responses of Julina (Olivia in the play), who is pregnant by the person she thought was Silvio, is one of Rich's wry touches, as she "did now thinke her selfe to be in a worse case than euer she was before, for now she knewe not whom to chalenge to be the father of her childe",[19] and she departs full of grief. It is only later that the real Silvio appears and in remorse returns to Julina. Meanwhile, the Duke's response to Silla's disrobing is first of all an emotional one – he is "amased" – and then he becomes aware of the moral implications of the situation, recognizing that Silla is "the branche of all vertue", that he has wronged her, and that her "liberalitie . . . can neuer bee sufficiently rewarded". Impressed by the love she has exhibited towards him, he "rewards" her patience by marrying her. The marriage is a result of Apolonius's perception into Silla's true worth. By displaying her womanhood, she has forced him to notice it. The news of the marriage, which "seemed so wonderfull and strange", spreads through Greece, and when Julina and Silvio are reunited, the former is "so rauished with ioye, that she knewe not whether she were awake, or in some dreame". A final sentence sums up the formal completion of the story:

> And thus, Silvio hauing attained a noble wife and Silla, his sister, her desired husband, thei passed the residue of their daies with such delight as those that haue accomplished the perfection of their felicities.[20]

The differences between the two accounts are important. Rich seems more interested in the intricacy of unravelling the knot, squeezing each incident dry for homely and ironic detail. The brisk narration of the ending shows that it is of less interest to Rich than the complicated manoeuvring during the courtship. Shakespeare's scene is built upon a simpler formula, but it is presented with much more lingering and patient attention before relaxing. His climax is also more richly amplified in its range of emotional responses, as each character sees the moment as a product of the past. There is Sebastian's poignant glimpse of the past:

> I had a sister
> Whom the blind waves and surges have devour'd:
> (V.i.220–1)

while Viola fears her brother is a spirit, "come to fright us" (V.i.227–8), and she anxiously tries to corroborate the story by the physical evidence of moles and mathematical calculations. There is a third vital difference. Rich leaves no loose ends. His people are married for good reasons and live happily ever after. Viola in the play, however, projects the formal close into the future when she shall put on woman's clothing:

> If nothing lets to make us happy both
> But this my masculine usurp'd attire,
> Do not embrace me till each circumstance
> Of place, time, fortune, do cohere and jump
> That I am Viola.
> (V.i.241–5)

The Duke briefly acts as spokesman for the moral point of view when he says of Sebastian, "right noble is his blood", but then he frames his proposal to Viola, not in the rigorously moral terms of Rich's Duke, but in a more or less aesthetic desire to "have share in this most happy wreck" (V.i.258). He does not profess present love for her, only a desire to see her in woman's weeds when presumably he will love her. His final speech again draws attention to a problem evaded by the prose writer, that Viola cannot truly be Orsino's lover, or even a woman, until she dons a woman's clothes:

> Cesario, come;
> For so you shall be while you are a man;
> But when in other habits you are seen,
> Orsino's mistress, and his fancy's queen.
>
> (V.i.371–4)

Perhaps there is an implication here that Orsino has at last learned to restrain his self-indulgent feelings so that he can see the truth with an accurate eye (or does "his *fancy's* queen" spell danger?); or perhaps the point is the formal one, that the comedy will not properly end until the solemn combination shall be made, a quiet hint that the future is not so closed off and womb-like as Rich has made it sound.[21] It is a dramatic necessity for Viola to wait until after the play has finished to change her clothes and "become" a woman, but Shakespeare emphasizes the point in such a way that it reinforces the idea of a woman trapped inside disguise and a social identity. Rosalind escapes by going offstage and changing her clothes, before joining the new social pattern in a more limited role. Viola remains at the end, as throughout, trapped by the situation. One wonders momentarily about the position of Maria at the end, in the light of the opportunism and offhandedness of Sir Toby's drunken proposition, "Come by and by to my chamber" (IV.ii.69). We learn that he has married her "in recompence" for devising the joke on Malvolio (V.i.351), a sardonic reflection on the "reward" in the source. This betrothal seems to be based either on a drunken whim or upon a joke played on somebody else, neither of which seems a good basis, especially after Toby has already tried to make a match between Maria and Sir Andrew.

A further disquieting note is struck by Malvolio's parting snarl, "I'll be reveng'd on the whole pack of you" (V.i.364), throwing into relief the fact that part of the comic effect ("loude laughter" rather than "soft smiling" or delight) has been built upon the darkness of his imprisonment and his painful awareness, that either he is mad, or the world is. For a moment, the sympathy of Olivia turns upon the audience a strong hint that its glee at Malvolio's predicament has been as nasty as the trick itself:

> Alas, poor fool, how have they baffl'd thee!
>
> . . .
>
> He hath been most notoriously abus'd.
>
>   (V.i.356 and 365)

Our complicity in the practical joking is reflected in the uneasy reaction of Sir Toby's entourage who, quite safely detached in their capacity as onlookers, begin to acquire a conscience about Malvolio's suffering, as the drunkenness of night turns into the hangover of the morning after. Toby begins to wish he "were well rid of this knavery" and he, with Maria and Andrew, are absent from the final moments, perhaps in penitent hiding. Fabian tries to excuse his cronies by pleading the general happiness of the occasion:

> Good madam, hear me speak,
> And let no quarrel nor no brawl to come
> Taint the condition of this present hour,
> Which I have wond'red at.
>
>   (V.i.342–5)

None the less, Malvolio's threat has already forecast a "brawl to come" that is inescapable. As is the case with the major characters, Fabian is trying to evade the consequences that the brazen world holds, and he prefers to live in the old tales told by knitters in the sun. With slight uneasiness he explains the trick played against Malvolio:

> How with a sportful malice it was follow'd
> May rather pluck on laughter than revenge,
> If that the injuries be justly weigh'd,
> That have on both sides pass'd.
>
>   (V.i.353–5)

He suggests that Malvolio's pride alone has been hurt, and that his puritanical austerity, a threat to the "cakes and ale" of the comic world, deserved its fate. But Malvolio's parting cry lingers, and it refers to the future rather than the "justly weigh'd" moral deserts of the past.

Feste's song at the end is fragmentary in sense and equivocal in tone. The final verse cheerfully sums up the idea that the golden, fictional world is now closed, and that more unpleasant facts, held at bay during the play, await us:

A great while ago the world begun,
    With hey, ho, the wind and the rain;
But that's all one, our play is done,
    And we'll strive to please you every day.

As in the songs at the end of *Love's Labour's Lost*, we are tempted to see a disengagement from art leading the audience back to the reality outside the theatre. But there is a weary shrug in "But that's all one", as if the speaker hardly has the energy or the desire to draw into any rational relationship the vast distances of time outside the play and the limited existence of its characters. The disengagement in the *Dream* is much more gradual and gentle, equally generous to both worlds. In the first four verses of the song there is a sardonic and depressing progression from the foolishness of childhood's illusory delights, the suspiciousness of early manhood, post-marital ennui, and finally the drunken, vacuous head of middle age. To underline the wearily fatalistic outlook comes the refrain, "For the rain it raineth every day." It is impossible to pin a particular significance or meaning upon the song, but its atmosphere is one of disconsolate melancholy. It picks up a tone struck particularly in the jaded, spiritless, and post-drunken weariness of Sir Toby Belch at the end of the night of debauchery:[22] "I would we were well rid of this knavery . . . Come by and by to my chamber." It reminds us that the "going-on power of life" can be as depressing and meaningless as death itself, and that this is a devastating answer to the willed illusions of an "improbable fiction" (III,iv,122). Golden lads and girls all must, like chimney sweepers, come to dust.

IV The "problem" comedies

We can be schematic for a moment, and summarize those aspects of the romance ending which Shakespeare has adopted in his comic climaxes. Several elements dovetail to give not only the sense of narrative finality but of completeness on several levels. *Scenically*, the final episode includes as many of the characters who appear in the play as possible in an ensemble. In *narrative* terms, the event of betrothal allows the action to "end" in one sense while also creating some sense in our minds that it could potentially go on forever. *Emotionally*, the dominant feeling raised in the audience is wonder at the harmony achieved in social and personal terms, although this feeling can be more or less qualified. An *older person*, usually a duke, has some judicial and choric function, articulating for us the events which are clarifying. *Morally*, there is a sense of the triumph of virtue (as presented in the terms of the play) and the defeat of anticomic impulses, sometimes permanently, at other times in a disquietingly temporary way. And underneath these various formulae lies a pervasive attitude to time, the romance attitude that the fulfilment of the characters' quests for relationship is "for short time an endless monument", a transient resting place indeed, precious in its impermanence and fragility, and yet one whose significance has a wash fore and aft. Romance, as a genre unlike stage comedy, includes no final ending. It takes its central rhythm from the oscillations of a life as it is being lived, full of ups and downs, never fully consistent in its moral and emotional continuity. Crises and disasters are met and lived through, happiness alternates with grief, serenity of conscience is troubled by an occasional sense of error and even of sin. Survival and patience are necessary qualities in riding through the good and the bad with equanimity. And just as an individual can never know his own death as a moment dividing being from non-being, so the romance takes its nature from a recognition that its own pattern is potentially endless. We have seen Shakespeare's early comedies move more surely towards an explicit acknowledgment of these romance attitudes towards time and experience, as he experiments with the "endless ending" in different forms.

It has been noticeable, however, that as Shakespeare seeks to include a wider register of romance experience from the joyful to the distressing, his plays have come increasingly to challenge from within the particular form of stage comedy, defined in terms of the unequivocally happy ending, that we sometimes call "festive comedy". With *Twelfth Night*, he seems to be pushing against the formal constraints, implying that as much is excluded from the festive spirit as is included. We need not say that he is necessarily trying to present a more "realistic" ending, since all modes of literature may be realistic within their own figurative terms. He is, however, moving towards a use of romance which is not subsidiary to comedy but primary in itself. In the two "problem" comedies, *All's Well That Ends Well* and *Measure for Measure*, we find Shakespeare extending the disquieting hints at the end of *Twelfth Night*. He presents the action in such a way that we become conscious of the elements of manipulation and even a hint of tyranny, in the imposition of the comic ending upon a potentially endless representation of people's fictional lives. Currents are set flowing that have to be coerced into a neat pattern by the end, and the coercion must be exercised both within the play, by a character or group of characters (the King and Helena in *All's Well* and the Duke alone in *Measure for Measure*) and by the dramatist from above in plotting the narrative. The plays would be more conventional, less worrying, if the creator did not seem so clearly aware of the nature of such manipulation. His somewhat frustrating sense that the potentially endless narrative must somehow be formally concluded reveals itself in different ways in each play, and implies a more transparently sceptical attitude towards the happy ending. In the account that follows it is convenient for the overall argument of this book to look at *Measure for Measure* first, although by this I do not intend to imply any new theory about the dating of either play.[1] In many ways, *All's Well That Ends Well* points more surely to the later plays, while *Measure for Measure* looks back — although critically — upon the form of comedy which Shakespeare has accepted and used up to this point of his writing career.

The "problem" confronting us in *All's Well That Ends Well* and *Measure for Measure* is basically one of generic expectations. What *kind* of plays are they? Even though their endings are just as simply "comic" in construction as *The Comedy of Errors*, the texture of experience encountered during the plays is too thick, too darkly aware of insoluble moral and emotional problems, too close to impending disaster, to allow us to group them confidently amongst the romantic comedies. If Fletcher's definition of tragi-comedy, a play that includes "the danger, not the death"[2] be accepted, then the plays might well fit here, but the term is used also to encompass plays where there *is* the death, such as some of Beaumont and Fletcher's works, and where the ending is more arbitrary, more subject to the whims of the dramatist in trying to catch us out or surprise us. Shakespeare's two plays do not quite lie easily in this company since, despite all the resistances to easy solutions, the endings are intuited throughout, and the plays would be somehow "wrong" to end with a tragedy. The genre in which these plays more truly lie, judging from what we have already said about the full-blooded romance attitude towards life, is romance itself, and the plays give us more evidence of Shakespeare's experiments with an "endless ending" at the close of a play. G. K. Hunter pointed towards this approach, but his suggestion has been taken up by surprisingly few critics:

> There is a strong case for avoiding the traditional separation of "problem-plays" from "romances" and considering as a group the "later comedies" – *All's Well*, *Measure for Measure*, *Pericles*, *Cymbeline*, and the rest. Viewed in this context, much that seems perverse in *All's Well* begins to fall into focus: in particular, the handling of the dénouement shows a clear relationship to that in the other plays . . .[3]

To go a little further, I feel there is equally no need to cut off either the "problem" comedies or the "last plays" from Shakespeare's earlier work in romantic comedy, and the link between them all is the rhythm of romance itself. As the experiments continue, Shakespeare draws from his efforts an increasingly clear conclusion, at its most obvious in *The Tempest*, that morality itself is relative and equivocal, as endlessly open to qualification or extension as the romance ending itself.

It is misleadingly easy to think that the change of tone and atmosphere from the romantic comedies to the "problem" comedies comes from a change in Shakespeare's psyche or mood. It is safer to suggest that his material is different because his sources are different, and so the problems encountered in the plays, both for the dramatic craftsman and for the audience, are also different. In these plays, Shakespeare is drawing on romance through another medium — the Italian *novella*. Boccaccio, Cinthio, and in the drama Whetstone, are all using romance motifs, and the territory is anciently familiar, but their concentration is upon a limited selection of such motifs.[4] L. G Salingar, for example, in giving us detailed accounts of these plays in relation to their continental sources, has not even found it necessary to look futher back at the pool of romance from which they emerged.[5] Even the most superficial glance at these plays and their sources is enough to show that the central concerns, although they may occur in romances, are not in themselves necessary to the love-centered romance vision. Questions surrounding the bed trick, for example, involving all the legalistic logic-chopping, may be used in romance to raise suspense, or to validate the happy ending, but by and large, even in the *Arcadia*, they are used as a means towards reasserting true emotional affection and a positive optimism about the workings of benign providence. In the Italian tales and in these two "Italianate" plays by Shakespeare the questions seem much more an end in themselves, with quantities of love and optimism tagged on in a sometimes formulaic and unconvincing way. It may help us to focus on *Measure for Measure* in particular, by suggesting that the dynamism and energy come not from a positive ethic of love, where intrigue and manipulation are used to enhance our wonder and confirm our faith at the end, but from a concentration upon intrigue itself. In this play, in fact, we see Shakespeare in the process of temporarily withdrawing from romance, or at least, taking romance through a long, dark tunnel.

Measure for Measure is more written about and disputed than any of Shakespeare's comedies. The one thing we can say is that it *is* a comedy in one thing at least, its ending. As soon as we know that Claudio is alive, we know that comic providence will dictate the events at the end. The fact that such providence is in the hands of the Duke of dark corners does arouse real doubts which I shall describe later, and the mesh of intrigue during the action shakes our confidence in a *natural* rhythm of benevolence which works towards a comic ending. Yet it does turn out to be a comedy, resting as does *All's Well* upon particular romance motifs: the revelation of disguised identity and the bed trick. Apart from these facts, little else is certain, even the play's subject matter. To mention the two extremes, some take the play to be "about" ideas, whether of Justice or Mercy or of Christian redemption, and the two most notable exponents of this approach are J. W. Lever and Wilson Knight.[6] At the other end stand Harriett Hawkins and J. C. Maxwell, who regard ideas in the play as opportunistic devices, used to illuminate a set of eminently theatrical confrontations between people in extreme situations.[7] In making any statement on the play, it becomes unavoidable simply to declare one's allegiances to a set of assumptions concerning the level of interest on which the action of *Measure for Measure* is pitched, and thereafter to be consistent.

A modest starting point may be two passages from a fine and concise essay by Peter Ure, and I intend to drive these two directions until they meet at a certain point. One statement that Ure makes at the outset runs thus:

> The revival of the laws against sexual immorality has upset the trade in vice. Shakespeare treats even these traders with an imaginative regard which releases a common pattern of feeling: that it is "us" (ordinary people who get on as best they may) versus "them" (the unreasonable state, the inexplicable decisions of governors, embodied in this case, in Angelo).[8]

Later, and as a separate point, Ure speaks of "the guillotine of comedy" which produces the resolution "For Comedy, or

Providence, has now taken charge," and this happens in the actions of the Duke as he takes control. But after the Duke has shown himself to be not only morally questionable but also an ineffectual plotter, and a liar to boot when he tells Isabella that Claudio is dead, we cannot accept him as a character in a completely sympathetic and amiable way. It is Shakespeare as dramatist who creates the happy ending, and the Duke is simply his agent. The word which connects the two quotations, which Ure himself does not use, is *authority*. Many people during the play either accept authority or have it thrust upon them, and the human interest comes from their attempts to reconcile the contradictions they face, or to ignore threats to their own personal consistency when they are in a position dependent upon authority. At the end of the play the dramatist himself takes authority, and he faces exactly the sorts of problems encountered by his own characters. The play concerns the clash not only between "us" and "them" but also between "us" and "it", where the latter is authority robed in itself. In this sense, Angelo, Isabella, and the Duke may be at the same time among "them" and also among "us", and it is this paradox that makes so much in the play problematical and difficult to analyze simply as a body of ideas. At the end, the dramatist himself is exposed to the treacherous grounds which one walks who undertakes the mantle of authority, even if it is over his own creation. The word "ceremony" is used pointedly in *Measure for Measure*[9] as the active adjunct of authority, and at the end, when the prevailing intrigue is dropped in favor of the romance mode, the "ceremony" fits the authority of the comic manipulator but not necessarily the life pulsing in the play.

The play's concentration upon authority and its human consequences explains why not only the plot but also the atmosphere turn upon points of law and of status, upon evasion and quibbles, and upon questions concerning immorality, rather than upon such romantic matters as identity within relationship, or peace and harmony, or upon feelings which are positive inducements to moral action. In confirmation of such a general impression, we notice that the subculture of the play lies not in the hands of an honest artisan such as Bottom, nor in the law enforcement of a Dogberry, or even in the amusing antics of the faithful servant. It lies this time in the genuine "criminal under-world" among the pimps and whores and vagabonds. Right at the heart of the play is a location which spreads to include the workings of the mind, and to become an immensely powerful visual and conceptual symbol: the prison.

The prison comes to contain, however transitorily, extremes of personalities and moral qualities. Claudio, who in another play could have embodied consistently the faith in human love that we find in a Helena, is rendered impotent by his incarceration, restrained for "too much liberty" (I.ii.119), and he rubs shoulders with the irrepressible but lowly Pompey Bum, "a poor fellow that would live" (II.i.211). The ethos of the prison includes the wretchedly drunken Barnardine and the dignified compassion of the Provost. It is visited by the representative of the law in the Duke and by religion in the person of the novice Isabella and the Duke's disguise. Furthermore, each major character is to some extent defined in terms of voluntary constraints upon action which amount to metaphorical prisons. Isabella enters the novitiate in order to confine her feelings and actions to the purely religious, and promptly finds herself in situations that display her role to be too circumscribed to allow her freedom over decisions she must make. The Duke finds his disguise a frustrating restraint as well as a new liberty, since some of his plans go awry simply because he cannot assert the authority of his office; and of course he must suffer the insults of the waspish Lucio. Angelo wraps his past and his feelings in the gowns of legalism and puritanism, showing himself to be a perfect example of what a post-Freudian world would describe as repression. He even inhabits his own geographical retreat which eventually becomes his prison where he commits his fatal indiscretion:

> He hath a garden circummur'd with brick,
> Whose western side is with a vineyard back'd;
> And to that vineyard is a planched gate
> That makes his opening with this bigger key;
> This other doth command a little door
> Which from the vineyard to the garden leads.
>
> (IV.i.26–31)

Here Isabella promises to meet Angelo "Upon the heavy middle of the night". Even the syntax of the description demands the use of keys to open it as each line unlocks a different hiding-place. Throughout the play, in terms of action and of character, liberty and "license" stand on one side, imprisonment and restraint on the other, and the result is an all-pervasive sense of "an impediment in the current" (III.i.233) which prevents uninhibited expression or movement. Feelings and impulses are bottled up by the exercise of artificially limited moral ideals, centering upon religion (both Puritan and Catholic) and authority, and the result, at least in Angelo's case, is a shocking explosion of liberty tainted by its very emphasis upon prurient virtue. As Shakespeare mentions elsewhere, "Lilies that fester smell far worse than weeds" (Sonnet 94).

What is interesting here is not just that the plot and characters are defined in terms of liberty and imprisonment, but there is a peculiar sense in which the play itself may be conceived in the same terms. There is a strain of truly religious feeling that runs through the play, yet it is left untapped, as if religion itself is caught up in its trappings of form, dogma, and creeds rather than carried by feelings. There is the deep potential for the romance vision imaged in the silent figure of the pregnant Juliet and verbalized in Mariana's song, so hastily broken off:

> But my kisses bring again, bring again;
> Seals of love, but seal'd in vain, seal'd in vain.
>
> (IV.i.5–6)

The words have a resonantly orphic quality, the dramatist commenting obliquely upon his artefact. The potential for romantic feeling in the play is left dormant, "seal'd in vain". Throughout, there is a tension between an individual liberty and life which throbs beneath the surface, and which could have been activated by the exercise of the imaginative vision willing to act upon generous and optimistic feelings, but no character is allowed to impose such a vision on the play. There is no Rosalind, Viola, or Helena. From another point of view, the playwright imposes a more rigid control upon his "low" characters who are not given the room to move and fully to impose their vitality as, for example, in his presentation of Bottom or of Falstaff and his cronies. These characters are allowed only moments of frustrated rebellion, as when Pompey directs his outraged question to the arm of the law, "Does your worship mean to geld and splay all the youth of the city?" (II.i.219). At one point a character even rebels forcefully against the impositions of the plot and of the dramatist's delegated representative, the disguised Duke. Barnardine, in a moment of magnificent dignity, refuses to die simply to expedite the plot, and he chooses to make his prison cell not a constraint but a palace, served so well as he is by friends generous to his appetites:

> Friar, not I; I have been drinking hard all night, and I will have more time to prepare me, or they shall beat out my brains with billets. I will not consent to die this day, that's certain.
>
> . . .
>
> Not a word; if you have anything to say to me, come to my ward; for thence will not I today.   [*Exit*
> (IV.iii.49–59)

Measure for Measure presents romance very much on a leash. There are the conventions of the genre, the stock motifs, but none of the internal modes of perception that give warmth to the form. The place where the tension on the leash becomes most obvious is the ending. Truth is trapped in intrigue, and Isabella believes that it is only she who can see it:

> Then, O you blessed ministers above,
> Keep me in patience; and with ripen'd time, .
> Unfold the evil which is here wrapt up
> In countenance!
> (V.i.118–21)

The ambiguity of the Duke's position is that, although he is as close in function to the "blessed ministers above" as anybody in the play, he seems to be often colluding in the intrigue and refusing to help. There is a dark suspicion that, as "dramatist within the machine", his prime motive is to wait until the unveiling of truth may be carried out with maximum theatrical effect, when he may stun his audience with his own power and authority by revealing the disguise he has been adopting, unlike Rosalind who knows her revelation will trap her. It is wry to reflect that his own plans during the play have not always been a total success, since he makes several mistakes in assumptions and strategy when he is plotting in the prison. He has lied to Isabella about her brother's fate, and by now leaving the fate of Isabella in the hands of Angelo, he is running some risks, not for himself, but for her. He has not revealed his identity to Isabella, and even if he had, his new actions, wrapped in the gowns of authority, are hardly calculated to reassure her or even the audience in a play that consistently presents authority itself as a dubious and unreliable quantity. What, for example, would stop the Duke reverting to the role of tough ruler as soon as he adopts the outer trappings of power, following the model of Angelo?[10] It is by no means unprecedented for power to protect itself and its supporters, and loftily to change its allegiances away from truth and humanity on the accession to its own authority. But luckily for Isabella, it is in the Duke's own interests to draw attention to himself by creating a *coup de théatre* which will reveal himself in the adopted role of saviour. Then, in apportioning punishments and rewards, acting as grand inquisitor, he draws attention to his own self-regarding exercise of power by first adopting the hard-line tag, "measure for measure", and flattering himself by his capacity thereafter to soften in the individual case, dispensing mercy with as much condescension as he has dispensed what he calls "justice". Angelo and Lucio, after being condemned to death, are — to their horror — condemned to living in the trap of enforced marriages, and Isabella, after spending the whole play trying to avoid the company of men, and the problems relating to sexuality, is prey to an arrogantly olympian solicitation, no less salacious for its being politely couched:

> If he [Claudio] be like your brother, for his sake
> Is he pardon'd; and for your lovely sake
> Give me your hand and say you will be mine.
>
> (V.i.488–91)

Only Angelo himself could match such a cynical bargain over a brother's life. We do not hear Isabella's answer, but we have ringing still in our ears her vehement words to Angelo in the spellbinding scene in which he, too, solicits and blackmails her in terms no more blatant, in the name of his authority. Concerning the other romance machinery, we need only compare the genuinely affectionate and mutually submissive reconciliation between Basilius and Gynecia in the *Arcadia*[11] to realize how coolly and perfunctorily it is used in *Measure for Measure* to reunite the reluctant Angelo and the self-demeaning Mariana.

We need not adopt an extreme position, condemning the Duke for being a bad man and suggesting that the ending is more tragic than comic. The ending is totally comic in its formal organization, and the Duke is seen eventually to have been benevolent in his manipulations. It is possible to suggest that Shakespeare's attitude towards the Duke oscillates in a mildly *self*-critical way, if we accept the implicit analogy at certain points between the Duke and the dramatist. Hazlitt has a wonderfully judicious statement on the Duke, which sums up many of the audience's attitudes:

> As to the Duke, who makes a very imposing and mysterious stage-character he is more absorbed in his own plots and gravity than anxious for the welfare of the state; more tenacious of his own character than attentive to the feelings and apprehensions of others.[12]

The further point is that in the play's design it is "authority" itself which is so dubious, since it often places individuals in impossible dilemmas, forcing them to act against their better consciences. "Drest in a little brief authority", people in the play respond to the rival demands imposed by public justice, personal desire, and personal conscience. The result can be self-contradictoriness, as in Isabella's words to Claudio, or moral collapse, as in the case of Angelo, or the person may simply hide behind a role, like the Duke in his two personae of friar and authority-figure. Since the Duke is the "dramatist-in-the-machine", like Rosalind but without her fully romantic ethic, some of the dubiousness that plays about figures of authority inevitably rubs off on the playwright himself, especially when one of his characters, Barnardine, rebels against the plot. To some extent Shakespeare, by using the conventions and motifs of romance to produce the dénouement, but by eliminating the spirit of love, presumed virtue, and generosity, is revealing some uncertainty about the status of the conventions. Given the demands placed upon him by allowing us to expect a happy ending, he produces the events without full conviction as a somewhat arbitrary imposition of authority that comes from a role of comic dramatist, not from the feelings. If, as A. P. Rossiter suggests, the Duke lacks the "magnanimity" to make him fully trustworthy as an instrument of romantic providence,[13] then something of the charge can be levelled also at Shakespeare. There is much "cold gradation and well-balanc'd form" (IV.iii.99) in the ending. The Duke himself in fact, commenting on the trust invested in him by Mariana and with a slightly mocking and condescending tone, likens his own power of fulfilling people's wishes to the comparable power of the imaginative writer:

> Thousand escapes of wit
> Make thee the father of their idle dream,
> And rack thee in their fancies.
>
> (IV.i.61–3)

Coercion itself is a subject of the play, secretive intrigue is its strategy, as Pompey and Mistress Overdone have the life in them incarcerated, and Angelo and Isabella are shifted like chess-figures into the appropriate liaisons demanded by the genre. "Love", the most profound value in the world of romance, exists here in various forms: as coercive lust without sympathy, or as something loftily taken for granted as the prerogative of power, or as something to be victimized as Claudio the lover is imprisoned. It does not exist as affection, nor as an imaginative quality. Natural "virtue", the other pillar of the romance ethic, is represented under such extreme pressures that it becomes, in the figure of Isabella, confused and uncertain. In the figure of the Duke virtue becomes secretive, sometimes ineffectual, and sometimes peremptorily abrupt.

Measure for Measure is not, as some critics suggest, a cynical play (nor am I suggesting that it is in any way unsuccessful). It has too much genuine ebullience, and too much honest puzzlement about where the truth lies in the face of contradictory positions. But by the end there is an element of anger and frustration. The only sustained speech in the final scene that comes straight from the feelings instead of from the calculating intellect is Isabella's furious tirade as she realizes that when truth stands on the opposite side to law and authority, it is likely to be dismissed as madness:

ANGELO: And she will speak most bitterly and strange.
ISABELLA: Most strange, but yet most truly, will I speak.
    That Angelo's forsworn, is it not strange?
    That Angelo's a murderer, is't not strange?
    That Angelo is an adulterous thief,
    An hypocrite, a virgin-violator,
    Is it not strange and strange?
DUKE: Nay, it is ten times strange.
ISABELLA: It is not truer he is Angelo
    Than this is all as true as it is strange;
    Nay, it is ten times true; for truth is truth
    To the end of reck'ning.
DUKE: Away with her. Poor soul,
    She speaks this in th'infirmity of sense.

(V.i.38–50)

The "strangeness" of this ending is not heightened sense of wonder but something much more disquieting. However, perhaps to the surprise of Isabella and the audience, the Duke proves himself to be courteously correct to the rules, and out of his benevolent exercise of authority he reprieves the forces of truth, virtue, and (equivocally) love. By his use of romance furniture in an anti-romantic room, the dramatist has shown himself to be awkwardly like his own characters in authority, shifting the chairs about without considering too deeply who is sitting on them. He applies the "laws" of romance and comedy, but with only token and questionable "mercy", and without imaginative conviction. The one character who is totally reprieved is the indomitable Barnardine, and one feels that both the Duke and the dramatist recognize that he has somehow escaped their net. The fictions of romance, as they are allowed to sway the circumstances of the dénouement, end up being little more than another impediment in the current, or otherwise an expedient concession made after the predominant tone of intrigue has run its course. The concession is made in order to preserve the façade of negotiated harmony that marks the whole business of the ending.

In the endings to the plays we shall be examining from now on, there is one extension of the romance pattern which is extremely important. The elderly duke or king who watches or comments, so familiar in romance, is now no mere observer but a crucially feeling participant in the events of the ending. Such spokesmen for elderly experience, stirred by the occasion to nostalgia or philosophical reflection, stand at the center of the last plays. Pericles, Cymbeline, Leontes, and Prospero are all old men by the end of their plays, at their journey's end, and their happiness in the social harmony is heavily qualified by the knowledge that it may have come too late for themselves. They must hand over the glowing torch of life to the young: "Welcome hither, As is the spring to the earth" is Leontes' greeting to the young couple after sixteen years of estrangement and grief,[14] and the retrieval of his own lost wife is as vulnerable, as lent or leased to him as a warm memory. Paulina may perfunctorily be handed a new husband at the end of *The Winter's Tale*, but a primary tone is struck in her lonely dirge for a lost partner:

> I, an old turtle,
> Will wing me to some wither'd bough, and there
> My mate, that's never to be found again,
> Lament till I am lost.
>
> (V.iii.132–5)

In each of these plays, as we shall see, the triumph of consummated happiness is "placed" within a perspective that includes weary experience, a sense of loss, and a recognition that the present is a moving point that leads backwards and forwards into darker areas. Such moments, when elderly experience is temporarily rejuvenated, exist in a twilight time between day and night, "as the morning steals upon the night,

Melting the darkness".[15] The "endless ending," involving short time and long time simultaneously, is partially achieved through the presence of such figures.

Throughout *All's Well That Ends Well*, there is a clear distinction made between three age groups: old age, represented by the King and the Widow; middle age, represented by the autumnally gracious Countess and the fussy, waggish Lafew; and youth, personified mainly in the precociously mature Helena, in Diana who is constantly defined as above all "honest", and the immature Bertram. At least until the cure of the King in the second and third Acts, a constant emphasis is placed, particularly by the King, upon the apparent degeneration of the world from when he himself was young. His idolatrous praise of his dead contemporary, Bertram's late father, is presented as a potentially comic harking back to "the good old days", setting an impossibly high standard of virtue and personal merit which Bertram can never be expected to live up to. By the end of the play, the balance has been redressed in favor of youth, at least insofar as the King can admire Helena and Diana, who hold hope for the future. But the tone of the final episodes is dominated and burdened by the King's elegiac melancholy, combined with his determination to restore harmony and endorse love before it is too late.

The closing scene opens with the sense of loss, as described by the King, when Helena is apparently dead:

> We lost a jewel of her, and our esteem
> Was made much poorer by it; but your son,
> As mad in folly, lack'd the sense to know
> Her estimation home.
> COUNTESS: 'Tis past my liege,
> And I beseech your Majesty to make it
> Natural rebellion, done i' th' blaze of youth,
> When oil and fire, too strong for reason's force,
> O'erbears it and burns on.
> KING: My honour'd lady,
> I have forgiven and forgotten all. . .
>
> (V.iii.1–9)

The word "lost" rings through the words of the King, the Countess, and Lafew, and the notion of forgetting is equally powerful:

> Praising what is lost
> Makes the remembrance dear . . .
>
> . . .
> The nature of his great offence is dead,
> And deeper than oblivion do we bury
> Th'incensing relics of it.
>
> (V.iii.19–25 *passim*)

The old King, already saved once from despair and death, seizes upon a rare moment of reconciliation when "the time is fair again" to suggest that the past must simply be forgotten, in order to salvage some semblance of a happy ending:

> All is whole
> Not one word more of the consumed time.
> Let's take the instant by the forward top;
> For we are old, and on our quick'st decrees
> Th'inaudible and noiseless foot of Time
> Steals ere we can effect them.
>
> (V.iii.37–42)

The dramatist, as if prompted by his own character's willingness to forget the somber past, hastens, although with a lumbering mechanism, to his own happy ending of the plot. But the slightly grudging quality of the presentation of Helena's "resurrection" is consistent with the King's own attitude to time and momentary happiness. As Evarchus, the judicial Duke in the *Arcadia*, was reluctant to allow lucky accidents too easily to salve the consciences of errant young people, so Shakespeare's ending here refuses to compromise the pain of the tangled history or to obliterate all the injustices perpetrated by Bertram, in a sentimental, wholly festive ending. The King's words and his tone draw attention to the fact that a happy climax is at the discretion of the dramatist, and that his characters are all at the mercy of his capacity to forgive and forget. In emphasis of this point, to screw our gratitude the more willingly from us, the King is given not only the last lines in the dramatic design, but also the dramatist's last lines in an Epilogue:

All yet seems well; and if it end so meet,
The bitter past, more welcome is the sweet.

[*Flourish*

EPILOGUE

The King's a beggar, now the play is done.
All is well ended if this suit be won,
That you express content; which we will pay
With strife to please you, day exceeding day.
Ours be the patience then and yours our parts;
Your gentle hands lend us, and take our hearts.

[*Exeunt omnes*
(V.iii.326ff.)

The Epilogue is turned back upon the audience: the dramatist is asked to "please" us in contradictory ways, by giving us "strife" but also "content" and the fact that he can "strive" to do so is something which invites our gratitude or at least our applause. It is another of Shakespeare's statements of the quality of romance that even when an ending is reached, it is no ending, since we will demand also a continuing future, day exceeding day.[16]

Within the somber purview of the King is enacted the dénouement to the love plot which forms the central thread of the play. Narrative finality is achieved by the use of three age-old romance motifs:

(1) recognition, in the presentation of Helena;
(2) the ring, as a sign of identification;
(3) the bed trick, as it is explained to the ensemble.

Stated so baldly, the ending to virtually any comedy would appear to be hackneyed and conventional. Recognition is universal in romance, extremely common in comedy, and by no means unknown in tragedy, as we can see in Lear's recognition of Cordelia and in Kent's revelation of his identity. The ring, we have already seen in *The Merchant of Venice* and contemporary statements by critics, was already recognized in the 1590s as a convention so common as to be susceptible to parody on the stage. The bed trick, although almost unprecedented on the stage[17] occurs in many well-known Italian and English prose romances from Boccaccio to Sidney, and the fact that Shakespeare is here being a dramatic innovator perhaps shows through in the way that he needs to spell out each detail. (By contrast, Sidney uses similar machinery with greater economy in the *Old Arcadia*.) Whereas earlier plays emphasize the surprise of the events to spectators and audience, in this play Shakespeare drags out the explanation for each at inordinate length. The only suspense involved is *when* he will eventually get around to springing surprises which are immediately obvious to the audience. In contrast, it is remarkable how swiftly the surprising events are revealed at the end of *Twelfth Night, Much Ado About Nothing*, and *As You Like It*, where all is done in an incident. As in *The Merchant of Venice*, the length of the last scene draws attention to the artificial nature of its narrative basis. The presentation of conventions is not so much perfunctory, as it may be in *Measure for Measure*, but it is leisurely, and somewhat contrived. Nor does Shakespeare do much by way of poetic utterance to arouse "wonder" in his audience. Much of the business in the last Act, apart from the King's reflections, is conducted at the level of explanation and rationalization, and is not pitched to stir our emotional pulses. *All's Well* is not quite the poetically impoverished play that many see it as, but it is true that, by and large, much of the energy lies in the prose of the Parolles scenes, and the only points where the verse rises above the functional to something unique in its quiet, dignified cadences, its modest eloquence, are in the King's statements, and in the early scenes dominated by Helena in her role as healer. The potential for "wonder" is dressed in irony bordering on parody in Lafew's

> Mine eyes smell onions; I shall weep anon.
> Good Tom Drum, lend me a handkercher.
>   (V.iii.314–5)

The generally functional and uninspiring quality of the verse in the last scene is the main factor in making the King's words so powerfully central in contributing to a time-conscious mood, which is quite different from comic and romance celebration of timeless moments. Everything in the presentation of the ending conspires to emphasize the glibness and expedience of the tag, "all's well that ends well," and to italicize the tentativeness of the syntax in the capping lines:

> All *yet seems* well; and *if* it end so meet,
> The bitter past, more welcome is the sweet.
>
> (V.iii.326–7 my italics)

In this play, Shakespeare, like his own King, does not seem to believe fully in his ending, or perhaps in "happy endings" at all.

The doubts we might feel at the end of this play come partly from Shakespeare's choice of heroine and from the way he is using romance. Helena is a woman who consciously and conscientiously adopts and sustains the fundamental ethics extolled by romance. However, her beloved Bertram and the whole society in which he exists pose almost impossible resistances to the implementation of this ethic in action. The dramatist, by isolating Helena even against the man she loves, sets himself a problem which he can solve only by placing his finger on the scale, by imposing something upon the narrative to give Helena her happy ending. The somber scepticism and cautious optimism in the words of the King reflect a kind of choice made by the dramatist in organizing the ending:

> I am not a day of season,
> For thou mayst see a sunshine and a hail
> In me at once. But to the brightest beams
> Distracted clouds give way; so stand thou forth;
> The time is fair again.
>
> (V.iii.32–6)

The King by royal prerogative, and Shakespeare by dramatic fiat, are both, with some misgivings, endorsing the creed which Helena has lived by — that to see the best possibility imposes an obligation to create the best, when one has the power to do so.

Helena, in her role as "weakest minister", cures the King with no remedy but human faith and hope. Without naming God, she pins her hopes on an unnameable capacity for seeing a future even where there is no evidence to expect one:

> Oft expectation fails, and most oft there
> Where most it promises; and oft it hits
> Where hope is coldest, and despair most fits.
>
> (II.i.141–3)

She speaks of "Him" and of "heaven", and yet her message is not a specifically Christian one, in name or in spirit. Whether we speak of God, or of a self-confidence that is humanist in its central commitment, or of some benign providence, all that Helena does is to insist upon the desire to live and to conquer despair. In so doing, she is reasserting the ideology of romance as a genre. She uses nothing but words to inspire hope:

> But know I think, and think I know most sure,
> My art is not past power nor you past cure.
> KING: Art thou so confident? Within what space
> Hop'st thou my cure?
>
> (II.i.156–9)

And in answer to the King's question, Helena speaks of Christian God and pagan gods in the same breath, a breath of mesmeric chanting, invoking no deity, proclaiming no more than that the King will live if only he should wish to:

> Ere twice the horses of the sun shall bring
> Their fiery torcher his diurnal ring,
> Ere twice in murk and occidental damp
> Moist Hesperus hath quench'd his sleepy lamp,
> Or four and twenty times the pilot's glass
> Hath told the thievish minutes how they pass,
> What is infirm from your sound parts shall fly,
> Health shall live free, and sickness freely die.
>
> (II.i.160–7)

Hedged about in the context of despair and logic-chopping scepticism, such overt "Poetry" with its obtrusive rhymes and firm rhythms has a precarious status, but for the King it does the trick and he equates Helena and her words with "life":

> Methinks in thee some blessed spirit doth speak
> His powerful sound within an organ weak;
> And what impossibility would slay
> In common sense, sense saves another way.
> Thy life is dear; for all that life can rate
> Worth name of life in thee hath estimate:
> Youth, beauty, wisdom, courage, all
> That happiness and prime can happy call.

Thou this to hazard needs must intimate
Skill infinite or monstrous desperate.
Sweet practiser, thy physic I will try,
That ministers thine own death if I die.

(II.i.174–85)

To speak of this incident early in the play is not a digression from our subject, the ending, for it is Helena's attitude that directly creates the ending. Although well aware of the corrosive rationalism of a Parolles as he splits hairs about virginity, she is wilfully pinning her hopes on the imagination and on romance as alternative ways of looking at the same facts. Romance is based on a philosophy of "seeing the best" in other people, trusting that "all will be well", continually hoping even at the cost of consciously and irresponsibly ignoring pragmatic and unfavorable concerns. Benign providence — the happy ending — in this play depends not on the logic of a literary paradigm working itself through, convincing the audience of its emotional rightness, but on the energetic exertion of a special point of view adopted by the heroine against all the odds. At its simplest the romance point of view depends entirely on investing one's trust in the power of human love, patience, and imagination, and Shakespeare's refusal to specify a particular god is perhaps his signal that such a position of faith may be religious in the most comprehensive sense of the word.

In the love plot Helena is consistent to her faith in her own imaginative perceptions, against the evidence and even against the audience's perceptions. The play presents a conflict in terms of a "decision about life" made by its central character. It gives us a heroine who has faith in the capacity of romantic love to change the object of love, but the daring stroke is that the play allows her to invest this faith in a "rude boy". Bertram expresses no particularly coherent attitude to the world — he is just an attractive, overly status-conscious and opportunistic young man — but all his actions display impetuosity, deep fear of being pursued emotionally, and a readiness to aspire to the unattainable (Diana). Helena, on the other hand, consistently accepts the force of her love, even as she recognizes that it is the product of "imagination" (I.i.80), and she denies that there is any truth except the one we create for ourselves:

Our remedies oft in ourselves do lie,
Which we ascribe to heaven. The fated sky
Gives us free scope . . .

(I.i.202–4)

When she asks herself,

What power is it which mounts my love so high,
That makes me see, and cannot feed mine eye?
(I.i.206–7)

her answer must be that it is her imaginative perception, a
sense above "common sense", and her intuitive evaluation of
Bertram which cannot be shared with anybody else. She has
early misgivings when she laments the "pity" "That wishing
well had not a body in't Which might be felt" (I.i.169–70), but
she immediately revokes her sad sense of caution in a bold
determination to take responsibility for her life. In the course
that she follows which includes an amalgam of positive
affection, hard bargaining, and sensitive reticence, she lives
out the credo spoken by Shelley at the end of *Prometheus
Unbound*:

To suffer woes which Hope thinks infinite;
To forgive wrongs darker than death or night;
To defy Power, which seems omnipotent;
To love and bear; to hope, till Hope creates
From its own wreck the thing it contemplates.

Admittedly, there is a disturbing similarity between the
apparently unattainable aspirations of Helena for Bertram
and Bertram for Diana, and he himself voices a cynical comment that could equally be applied to Helena:

. . . all impediments in fancy's course
Are motives of more fancy . . .
(V.iii.212–3)

Similarly, when he thinks he has lost Helena finally, repro-
achfully confessing his newly acquired love for her, he explains the change in terms which are close to Helena's insistence that one's imaginative conception of another person can
either   distort   or   beautify   the   physical   impression

(V.iii.45–54). There is no absolutely convincing way to explain away such disturbing parallels, but it seems fair to say that Helena throughout is placed on a different side of the moral fence, expressing virtue, constancy, and creative imagination, while Bertram is fickle, cruel, and destructive. Furthermore, it is made pretty clear at various points of the play that at least until his late "conversion" (however unsatisfactory this word may be), Bertram's eyes are fixed not on Helena's worth as a person, upon her inner qualities, nor even upon her physical attractiveness which so entrances Lafew. He sees only her social status, while Helena's eyes and imagination are held by something that "passes show" in him, and upon personal qualities which we must simply take on trust as being true for her. Shakespeare has given us other worthy heroines paired with unworthy heroes (Julia and Proteus, Hero and Claudio, and perhaps Viola and Orsino), but he has not made the heroine so closely akin to the dramatist himself in manipulating events until they produce the desired or generically appropriate result. The other heroines (even Rosalind) are at the mercy of their comic worlds, for they simply need to be patient until time, accidents, history draw them to the ark of the comic ending. Helena does the work herself with some support from the Countess and the King, and the sense of strain and of almost mercenary negotiation that lies behind her necessity to make a *bargain* to marry Bertram provides a metaphor in the story for the strain which the dramatist must exert in making his bargain with the disagreeable facts in life before he can create the happy ending.

The metaphor of the commercial bargain fully surfaces in the language of the final scene, in contrast to the language of miracles in the scene in which Helena cured the King. Lafew, on discovering Bertram's treachery, exclaims "I will buy me a son-in-law in a fair, and toll for this" (V.iii.145). Diana protests her virtue in terms denying that she can be bought as a common gamester:

> He does me wrong, my lord; if I were so
> He might have bought me at a common price.
>
> (V.iii.187–8)

But in order to prove her claim she argues that she was bought, but at a much higher price. She produces the ring "Whose high respect and rich validity Did lack a parallel" (V.iii.190–1). This is enough to convince the Countess:

> He blushes, and 'tis it.
> Of six preceding ancestors, that gem
> Conferr'd by testament to th' sequent issue,
> Hath it been ow'd and worn. This is his wife:
> The ring's a thousand proofs.
>
> (V.iii.193–7)

There is more business with the ring to follow, and its function, as in *The Merchant of Venice*, is both spiritual, standing for fidelity and ancient values, and commercial, putting a price on a relationship. As in *The Merchant*, there is a special significance in such a use of the old romantic talisman. Both Portia and Bassanio were forced in different ways to defend their love in the marketplace, and in *All's Well* neither Bertram nor Helena is quite free of the charge of buying love, Helena with the action of curing the King and Bertram with the ring and an oath. There is a curious sequel in the train of commercial imagery as Diana produces Helena with the claim that she is a jeweller who will give her "bail" and "surety" on the value of the ring. In fact when Helena appears, the tone is one of muted wonder, but behind the amiable surface the metaphor is still present: Helena has pawned the ring and is now reclaiming it. Both she and Bertram have pawned a marriage with Diana acting as broker, and they are now redeeming it. "All's well that ends well" is the philosophy of the market-place, for if one gets a bargain the price is justified. Sardonically, the play does not eliminate such logic.

Another peculiar and equally unromantic characteristic of *All's Well* is the explicitness of its preoccupation with sexual matters. The conventional heroine from romance is quite capable of putting up a spirited and frank defense of her right to remain a virgin, but never does she argue for her right *not* to be a virgin as does Helena: "How might one do, sir, to lose it to her own liking?" (I.i.141–2). At least she does not discuss the matter in such graphically physical detail with a disreputable character like Parolles. Similarly, although the bed trick is used in romances from the *Arcadia* to *Measure for Measure*, the heroine is never so personally ruthless in effecting it. (In fact, as in Isabella's case, the heroine is usually not the bed partner herself.) Even in Shakespeare's plays, no romantic hero (not even the dubious Troilus or Posthumus) is so grubbily committed to a creed of sexual pleasure without responsibility, the soldier's careless wenching. Bertram boasts with relish to his comrades of his conquests. The significance of such a dwelling upon the physical and seamy side of sex appears to be connected with the title of the play. Helena first voices the sentiment to the Widow after playing her part in the bed trick:

> Our waggon is prepar'd, and time revives us.
> All's Well That Ends Well. Still the fine's the crown.
> Whate'er the course, the end is the renown.
>
> (IV.iv.34–6)

She has continuously worried about the morality of expediency in such matters, the possibility of "wicked meaning in a lawful deed" (III.vii.45), and she can be absolved from any guilt in effecting her lawful purposes. Bertram, without her scruples, cannot be condoned. The means adopted by both may be very similar, but it is the end which matters when adjudicating the moral deserts. Shakespeare has here given a much more searching presentation of the problems involved in sexual morality as early as *The Two Gentlemen of Verona*. The problems are inherent in the stuff of romance, but by demonstrating them with such rigor, the playwright has taken us some distance from the spirit of romance.

To return to our central point, the dramatist in *All's Well* is rewriting Rosalind's story, but with crucial differences. It must be enacted in the urban world instead of a benign forest, and worse still, Helena's love-object, although just as young and callow as Orlando, does not love her. In giving dramatic form to such a conception, Shakespeare has set himself many problems of design in this play, for our generic expectations do not prepare us for such a "dramatist-in-the-machine." By giving us a worthy heroine in an unworthy world (instead of in a golden world of romance which will condone and naturally effect her purposes), he runs the risk of making the bargain too hard-won for our endorsement, of making it Helena's ending,

and not the audience's. Helena reaps her reward, but because
of our own necessarily unsympathetic attitude to Bertram and
our sense that he is "not good enough for her" the victory
seems precarious and perhaps hollow. But however sceptical
we may be about this ending, the problem lies in the
ambitiousness of the undertaking. Shakespeare has presented
romance and the sense of the "happy-ending", not as plot
devices but as beliefs, a self-sufficient way of looking at, and
eventually changing, the life around us. He is to take the same
risk in giving to Cleopatra such a myth-making eulogy of
Antony, and at least in the latter case he is to succeed
triumphantly so far as the enterprise will allow him. The last
words on the particular kind of endless ending employed by
Shakespeare in *All's Well*, full of fears about the past and the
future and full of moral relativities, may be taken from the
mouths of two admirable but unsung choric figures, the *almost*
anonymous French lords who happen to be brothers. (At least
one, perhaps both, are dignified with a name.)[18] Generally
speaking, they are trustworthy commentators, the more so
because they are disinterested, and there is a quality in their
perceptions that clarifies the equivocations not only of other
characters but of the dramatist himself:

> SECOND LORD: I am heartily sorry that he'll be glad of this.
> FIRST LORD: How mightily sometimes we make us comforts
> of our losses!
> SECOND LORD: And how mightily some other times we
> drown our gain in tear! . . .
> FIRST LORD: The web of our life is of a mingled yarn, good
> and ill together; our virtues would be proud if our
> faults whipt them not; and our crimes would despair if
> they were not cherish'd by our virtues.

(IV.iii.61–71)

The critic, uncertain how to evaluate the final scene and
tempted to overestimate or underestimate its dramatic skill,
would do well to ponder the lines and take them to heart as a
description of the area of human dealings encountered in the
play as a whole.

It is not unknown for writers to allow their works, or their titles, to make a conscious or semiconscious comment on the stage of creative development which they have reached. At the simplest level, Spenser's "Colin Clout's Come Home Again" is recognizably biographical of the poet's disillusioned return to court. Sidney's *Arcadia* was written while he was living on his sister's country estate in enforced, contemplative rusticity. Milton titled *Paradise Lost* in a mood of bitterness, in prison, and in fear of assassination, after the profound disappointment of seeing his own hope for an Utopia, the Commonwealth, had been lost;[19] and the world of his "prompted song", *Paradise Regained*, is an internalized struggle with the devil, an attempt to win a peace within which can no longer be achieved without, and to retrieve hope out of the jaws of despair. Yeats, in the significant year of 1914, decisively turned from the imaginative romanticism of the world of the Celtic twilight towards a new set of subjects and attitudes in a volume significantly called *Responsibilities*. It may seem too schematic to suggest that Shakespeare, in his "problem" comedies, and particularly in *Measure for Measure*, is similarly describing a phase of his own creative development: but the titles themselves, with their laconic, generalizing tone, implying a certain scepticism towards the plays as artefacts and towards the audience as consumers, allow us to make something of the idea. If the Duke in the latter play is somehow closely connected in his watchfulness and his manipulations with a dramatist in precarious authority over his own characters and plot, then the unconscious metaphor can be extended. The Duke, at first lax and popular, is looking for a way to set a precedent for a new rigor, and he creates the authority of Angelo and his own disguise in order to cloak the change in his own attitude to the state. Hence, the action of reprieving people from full punishment for their actions may be seen as "mercy" rather than as indulgent softness. Shakespeare, popular as the "mellifluous and honey-tongued" and "witty" writer of 1598[20] known primarily for his comedy, histories, and the romantic tragedy of *Romeo and Juliet*, has been gradually disengaging himself from unequivocal endorsement of the conventional, comic ending, and he needs to create for himself an opportunity to communicate a harsher, essentially tragic view of a world in which laws of "poetic justice" will mean something firm, unbendable, and dark. It is not necessarily Shakespeare's feelings about his own *life* which lead him to write these plays: we need not return to the view of Dowden and Chambers who felt that he was undergoing a breakdown at this time simply because, as mentioned, he has chosen to use a new kind of source material. But the "problem" comedies certainly reflect a new attitude on Shakespeare's part towards his own art and towards the version of romance which has been his stock-in-trade up to 1600. They reflect not only a glimpse of what he is about to achieve in his tragedies but also an acknowledgment of what he is losing in now expressing a sense of confinement and even disillusionment in the conventional employment of the comic ending.

V Romance in the tragedies

All's Well and *Measure for Measure* show some uncertainty in Shakespeare's mind about how he can choose to utilize the motifs of romance. Drawing upon romance at secondhand through the Italian tale of intrigue,[1] he discards much of the romance ethic and atmosphere, while employing some of its characteristic narrative events. *Measure for Measure* comes close to expressing scepticism about the mode of romantic comedy which Shakespeare has previously employed to encapsulate the wonder of the endless ending. This play's ending looks suspiciously like a facile literary formula, a naked imposition of the authority of generic expectations. Characters seem to be at their most vital and interesting when they are up to no good, rather than when they are exercising the virtues that spring from emotional generosity. *All's Well* salvages some of this generosity, but by investing it in one character who stands almost alone, the ending risks being "happy" for Helena but for nobody else. None the less, although this play also shows Shakespeare's faith in romance slipping a little, the idea that one character, by seeing the best, may eventually create a better world through the power of optimistic vision, provides a seam that will re-emerge later to create a different form of dramatized romance in Shakespeare's late works. Since this book deals primarily with the comic manifestations of romance, evidenced by the "happy" ending, we can afford ourselves only the briefest comments on the interim tragedies.

Much blood flows under the bridge in the next six or seven years of the canon as Shakespeare engages himself fully with tragedy. Romance tends to go underground except for occasional and relatively optimistic moments. It is necessary to remind ourselves, however, that the use of romance material in tragedy is by no means Shakespeare's innovation. Throughout its long history, romance has provided stories with unhappy endings as well as happy, with Troilus and

Cressida, Hero and Leander as the ones mentioned most often in Shakespeare's own plays.[2] If Fortune overrules Providence, then death, and not marriage or reconciliation, may provide the end of the story. Sidney's *Arcadia* has come perilously close before being whisked into the comic world by timely events. However, it is not simply the story but the writer's treatment which creates a romance. We can see this immediately by glancing at the total contrast between Shakespeare's two tragedies which use romance as the basis, *Romeo and Juliet* and *Troilus and Cressida*.

Romeo and Juliet is almost wholly romantic in its vision and conventions, and the tragic ending partly reflects the capacity of the romance writer to stop more or less whenever he likes. Although infinitely more skilful than the old *Common Conditions*, and better prepared, the ending here is, in kind, rather like its clumsy predecessor since it stops at the moment of death without going on to give us a mutual rebirth of both lovers. *Pyramus and Thisbe* is a parody of the form even down to its moral tag that "the wall is down that parted their fathers". More than this, the ending of *Romeo and Juliet* is suffused with the vision of romance as the lovers are united through death in a way that subsumes the tragic accidents: they are together forever in consummation of their total love. It is only when Shakespeare can will himself back into this frame of mind — and he does so in a great divine comedy of mature, middle-aged love, *Antony and Cleopatra* — that he can return with his faith restored to follow the path of ancient romance. Only when he can convince himself that romance is capable of celebrating and transcending death, as well as young love, can he again invest his trust in its modes.

Romeo and Juliet draws upon the central concept in romantic tragedy, the spirit of *liebestod* in which lovers are only united truly in death. This is not contradicted but proved by the fact that apart from their brief night of love the characters are repeatedly separated whilst they are living, even to the extent that "sour misfortune's book" dictates that they do not die in a living embrace but at different times. It is important to the myth of the immortality of young love which Shakespeare is creating that only after they have left the mortal world can there exist an inviolate unity between the two people who in life have been forcibly held apart. The "tragic scene" is also enacted in Shakespeare's paradox of the phoenix and the turtle:

> . . . How true a twain
> Seemeth this concordant one!
> Love hath reason, reason none,
> If what parts can so remain.
> ("The Phoenix and the Turtle", lines 45–8)

A similar paradox is presented in many of the most affirmative poems of John Donne:

> We can die by it, if not live by love,
> And if unfit for tombs and hearse
> Our legend be, it will be fit for verse.
> ("The Canonization", lines 28–30)

Shakespeare in *Romeo and Juliet* is engaged in creating a "legend" of the "canonization" of young love, and the success of his enterprise is measured by the fact that "Romeo and Juliet" more or less as a single entity takes its place with "Tristan and Isolde" and "Heloise and Abelard" as a supreme fact in the history of love. It is debatable whether such a triumph could have been effected by the existence of the mere sources upon which he built. More pertinently, Shakespeare invests his story with such a potency over the popular consciousness by drawing upon all the facets of the romance ending which we have noticed. Death is arbitrary and yet it is conclusive, an endless ending. Wonder as well as pathos illuminates the final scene as brightly as Juliet's beauty lights up the darkness of the vault in the early morning:

> Here lies Juliet, and her beauty makes
> This vault a feasting presence full of light.
> (V.iii.85–6)

Finally, as well as creating a lasting monument to love, the final scene has healthy moral consequences for the future in the mortal world.

Troilus and Cressida is quite different in tone, despite the similarity in its romance origins. Shakespeare was given several options by his various sources, and he chose to take the most unexpected course, challenging the generic expectations fundamentally. Without forfeiting the impulse of romance he could have followed in Chaucer's footsteps, preserving the poignant but beautiful brevity of young love even while casting a rueful, experienced eye upon its inbuilt dangers:

> Swich is this world, whoso it kan byholde:
> In ech estat is litel hertes reste.
> God leve us for to take it for the beste!
> (*Troilus and Criseyde*, V.1747–50)

Chaucer, by his own admission, seeks to create his plangent tone of regret and pity by relegating the whole issue of the Trojan war to the background, concentrating instead upon the love affair itself, using all his lyrical poetry in celebration of the rare moments of happiness. It is with distaste but little real condemnation that he presents the infidelity of Criseyde, and he leaves it to others to follow the story into the more brutal area of the war. Shakespeare, on the other hand, brings the war to the forefront, and the central interest lies in the disastrous emotional and moral consequences for individuals when two states are engaged in a pointless and degrading war fought over the abduction of a woman who is regarded more as a trophy than a person. The part of the story dealing with Troilus and Cressida recedes in importance, and is presented in the context of the dishonorable politics of war. In such a focus, nobody emerges with any credit, and love itself is debased.

A useful term to apply to *Troilus and Cressida* might be "satiric tragedy", a kind of contradiction in terms, for we normally associate satire with humor while tragedy deals with life in terms of high seriousness. In this play the rhetoric used by characters may be heroic, tragic, and romantic, but the whole presentation serves to undermine the lofty words by the baseness of actions. The heroic aspirations of the tragic protagonist, expressed through the figure of Hector as he is seen by others, are ruthlessly undercut, not only by the humiliating way in which he dies, but in his own actions when he turns his back on his own verbalized principles, and agrees to hunt with the pack of young, impetuous dogs in pursuing an unjust war.

The hollow ineffectuality of his principles precludes us from investing sympathy in his actions. The high-flown values of the romantic lover, Troilus, are made impotent when he is cuckolded and left flailing with outrage:

> Never did young man fancy
> With so eternal and so fix'd a soul.
>
> . . .
>
> O Cressid! O false Cressid! false, false, false!
> Let all untruths stand by thy stained name,
> And they'll seem glorious.
>
> (V.ii.163–4, 176–8)

Beneath such a rhetorically moving statement lies another irony, since it is at least arguable that Troilus's loss was not caused conclusively by Cressida's falsity but by the fact that his own motives in involving himself in love had been questionable from the beginning. The *actions* of a man who plots for love, who easily acquiesces in the decision to send his lover to the enemy camp as a vulnerable hostage (in a war fought over an enforced hostage, Helen), and who precipitately leaves the bed of love with a whispered order to the messenger that he must not be known to have slept with Cressida, are hardly the transparent actions of one who *says* he has loved "with so eternal and so fix'd a soul". In his actions in this personal relationship Troilus reveals himself as treacherous, hypocritical, and willing to betray his lover at the earliest opportunity. Similarly, the "romantic" heroine, after speaking hyperboles about love and constancy turns out to be, at least in the eyes of some people, a clever coquette with a practical eye for the convenient chance. On the other hand, we should be aware that Cressida is never *allowed* to make her actions square up with her rhetoric, for in this harsh, male-dominated world (perhaps best revealed through the cold wittiness of Helen, the "prize" herself) the woman has no choice. "You men will never tarry" (IV.ii.16) is a haunting note, which should remind us that love, in the romance sense, full of generosity, faith, and commitment is never even given a chance to prove itself in such a war-like, competitive, and brutal society. We in the audience cannot condemn Cressida for her actions, since they are largely determined from without. By maligning her as most critics do,[3] we are, like Hector, hunting with the mad pack, endorsing and perpetuating their cynical dismissal of the alternative values of virtue, love, and co-operation. The most perceptive, if ruthlessly hardened, commentator on this brazen world of hatred and accidents, is Thersites, but rather than posing a more healthy set of values to set against the shabby world of personal and public politics, he gleefully indulges his own savagely disillusioned idealism: "Lechery, lechery! Still wars and lechery! Nothing else holds fashion. A burning devil take them!" (V.ii.194)

In a temporary lapse of his characteristic touchstones of forgiveness and generosity, Shakespeare has chosen to mock any human utility in "seeing the best", and he has dehumanized all appeals to love, courage, and patience, by making them appear ludicrously inappropriate to the world as it is. If *Measure for Measure* casts a cold eye on the literary artifice of romance, *Troilus and Cressida* mauls its very *raison d'être*. But like a good master, Shakespeare is not long distrustful of his servant. In some of his tragedies, he gradually regains confidence in the romantic vision, and he moves more purposefully towards the position that although the world itself may be brazen, individuals can with faith in their benevolent instincts see it as golden, and retrieve for the survivors a form of idealism.

The process can be traced in *Othello*, where Shakespeare plays out to the bitter end a struggle between two fundamentally opposed visions of the world embodied in Iago and Desdemona respectively. While the former represents something like the destructive prejudices of "public opinion", plausible, rationalistic, and unillusioned, the latter lives her life by qualities of unquestioning trust and absolute commitment to a generous perception of her lover: "I saw Othello's visage in his mind" (I.iii.252). Desdemona never wavers but Othello in his rapid degeneration from a similar commitment ("My life upon her faith" I.iii.294) is putty in Iago's hands, gradually shaped into the inarticulate, sub human creature which was Iago's initial, repulsively racist preconception, an "old black ram" (I.i.89), a "devil" (I.i.92). Although appealing constantly to such reasonable, socially necessary values as service, money, and common sense, Iago

is as wrapped up in the folds of illusion as any romantic lover
and his illusions happen to be destructive rather than creative.
That Shakespeare is consciously placing Othello in the middle
of a genuine and fundamental moral confrontation appears
from a contrast between his play and his source. Cinthio's
story was one of intrigue and harshness, and from his presentation Shakespeare has found and developed the volatile,
male-dominated atmosphere of a military garrison where
women, by their very scarcity, are treated as commodities
(Bianca), as faintly ridiculous (the middle-aged Emilia), or as
angels (Desdemona) whose imputed sexuality acts only as a
source of fear and challenge to the soldier who wants nothing
better than to debase and possess such a woman even in the
triviality of forcing her to respond to bawdy jokes
(II.i.103–80). What Shakespeare adds to his source, as a
compensation and a radical development are the wonderfully
assertive and dignified lines by Desdemona in declaring her
love for Othello, and the premonitory pathos of the scene in
which she sings the "willow" song and muses sadly upon the
source of her predicament, "these men, these men!"
(IV.iii.58). The analogy may sound surprising, but
Shakespeare's treatment of his source in *Othello* is the same as
that in *The Comedy of Errors*. He has added sentiment and the
values of romance to a tale which was signally unsentimental.

In fact, to take the analogy between Shakespearean comedy
and this tragedy a little further, the dramatist provides in
Othello a tragic equivalent to the endless ending of romantic
comedy. Although death is far more final and decisive than
marriage, Shakespeare draws out to remarkable length the
death of Desdemona, as if to give Othello more time to repent.
The terrible train of events that lead to her death begin in
earnest as early as IV.iii, the "willow" scene, when Desdemona, although full of forebodings, reasserts her love:

> . . . my love doth so approve him
> That even his stubbornness, his checks, his frowns —
> Prithee unpin me — have grace and favour in them.
> (IV.iii.18–20)

She pleads that her wedding sheets should be her shroud, a
sign that she wishes to create imaginatively the happy ending

of comedy which now she realizes is impossible. Then in Act Five the time taken by Othello to smother her prolongs both the pain and the opportunity for last minute reprieve from a situation just as manipulated and contrived, based upon accident, as anything in comedy. The actual death is equally agonizing, as Desdemona, so far as the audience is aware, comes back to life, for after apparently dying on the words "O Lord, Lord, Lord!" (V.ii.87) she revives some sixty lines on to provide a moment of stillness and the beauty of self-sacrifice in the midst of noise and violence:

DESDEMONA: O, falsely, falsely murder'd!
EMILIA: O Lord, what cry is that?
OTHELLO: That! What?
EMILIA: Out and alas! that was my lady's voice.
     Help! help, ho! help! O lady, speak again!
     Sweet Desdemona! O sweet mistress, speak!
DESDEMONA: A guiltless death I die.
EMILIA: O, who hath done this deed?
DESDEMONA: Nobody. I myself. Farewell.
     Commend me to my kind lord.
     O, farewell!   *[Dies*
(V.ii.120–8)

Whereas Lear hopes against hope to find breath on the lips of the dead Cordelia despite that the text gives no cause for optimism, the audience could be forgiven for actually expecting a revival of Desdemona, for she has come back from death once or perhaps even twice. The main point is that the qualities she represents live on in the mind. Unfortunately, we must equally notice, Iago is not dead at the end of the play, so that the struggle between the radical opposites of good and evil will still continue.

Tragedy is a "foregone conclusion" (III.iii.432) after Othello abandons his trusting conception of Desdemona, and the play demonstrates how vulnerable the conception is in a hostile world. But we do find love's ability to light up the world temporarily as an imaginative force. Othello's love may be turned into hatred, and Desdemona, "moth of peace", the quiet, patient lover, may be destroyed, but what their visions

of each other at the beginning represent remains as an ennobl-
ing, spiritual quantity that rescues something of value from the
worldly destruction of their love. To prove the point that it is a
person's imagination that creates his world, we notice that
Iago's interpretation of events, self-evidently an effective one, is
based just as much on a self-generated illusion as love itself. He
proves Helena's rule which Othello tragically forgets, that we
may take control over our lives if we choose to exert imagination and trust in a vision. The tragedy for all is that Iago's
imagination chooses to fasten on the worst, and thereby helps
to create the worst. Events in a play are transmuted into
patterns for us only by the illusions of powerful imaginations,
and the struggle in *Othello* clarifies an intellectual dilemma
which Shakespeare has followed through several plays. Romance and satire are the true natural enemies, not comedy and
tragedy. In this play satire wins pragmatically, but romance
wins a Pyrrhic victory by leaving traces of a spiritual potential
for beauty and love which, the moral imagination cries out,
should be implemented in the world. In taking the force of this
insight, we are moving towards Shakespeare's resuscitation of
true romance in his last plays.

King Lear is one tragedy in which romance elements have
been recognized and explored by recent critics, most expertly
by L. G. Salingar.[4] Ever since the eighteenth century
adaptation by Nahum Tate (or, indeed, since the time of
Shakespeare's own sources), it has been accepted that *Lear*
could have been given a happy ending without drastically
upsetting the structure, and the source of such a notion is the
existence within the play of romance elements and expectations.

King Lear uses romance in all the ways we have explored in
this book, first as a range of imaginative attitudes that may
make reality different for the perceiver and secondly as a set of
literary motifs and expectations that determine the nature of
the audience's involvement in a play. When Lear is quieter
and more humble in the presence of Cordelia at the end, it is
partly the awareness of her silent love that has changed him.
In a dark world of ferocity and wilderness characters are able
at rare and precious moments to warm themselves at the
embers of another's sympathy. The act of living is seen as a

journey through purgatory made bearable only by the willing exercise of the imagination in extending compassion and tenderness — by a quantity that is "nothing" and everything at the same time. Just as it has been said that *King Lear* is "a Christian play about a pagan world",[5] so we may say that it is a hopeful play set in a hopeless world, and it is romance that adds hope. Some characters like Gloucester and Edgar are able to find hope in a manner dangerously close to reliance upon platitudes, while Cordelia, Albany, and Kent provide the fuel, respectively, of uncompromising and silent love, moral outrage, and feeling pity. The Fool, by limiting his concern to the adversity of his own uncomfortable condition, cuts himself off from the worst mental anguish and is attentive to the basic needs of his master while continually reminding Lear of his moral error. Edmund, Goneril, and Regan can maintain an Iago-like point of view, seeing the worst and, by the act of perceiving, creating the worst, although even the two women do it in hope, trying to win the heart of Edmund. They wish to prove themselves worthy members in "the ranks of evil". Lear treads a path between egotistical self-pity and an all-embracing humanity which can, in flashes of insight, divine the hardships of "poor naked wretches" that bide the pelting of the pitiless storm. In his oscillating self-interest and selflessness he is the measure of mankind in dealing with the adversities of this world. The audience, involved to the extent that it can find no easy answers in a play that provocatively tempts us with answers only to snatch them away, must rest content in seeing "feelingly", and concluding that events in themselves have no malevolence, but that man's imagination in malignity or hope can find its own answer according to its question and according to the need of each individual.

In many ways, the responses of Kent and Edgar are the ones that point us most directly to the way romance is being used in the play. These two characters stand almost as literary critics (or as ineffectual dramatists in disguise) inside the work, basing their expectations upon literary precedents reinforced by a firm, if simple, grasp of moral values. Kent is the one who understands that in the decorum of a romance (such as Sidney's *Arcadia*) a king who abdicates will set his kingdom to ruin, but that he will eventually be reinstated and restore stability, and he awaits the assertion of such a pattern: "Fortune, good night, smile once more; turn thy wheel." (II.ii.168) Although invoking fortune, he is really calling upon the benign goddess of Providence who rules romance and comedy. He is the one who "almost sees miracles" (II.ii.160) in the condition of misery. He knows his part in such a drama — to disguise himself and be patient, like Julia, Viola, and Helena — and there seems so little pragmatic reason for his disguise after a certain point that it is valid to see his retention of it as an artificial response to a literary paradigm. He is the one who awaits "the promis'd end" (V.iii.263). But it is he who, at the end of the day, admits that such expectations have come to nothing: "All's cheerless, dark, and deadly" (V.iii.290), and his last words imply he has decided that he is not a character in a romance but one in a Roman tragedy, and that he has another rôle to play now:

> I have a journey, sir, shortly to go.
> My master calls me; I must not say no.
> (V.iii.321–2)

Edgar relies upon even more rigid literary expectations, knowing that in a conventional work evil may temporarily hold sway over good but that poetic justice will eventually restore the balance:

> The lamentable change is from the best;
> The worst returns to laughter.
> (IV.i.5–6)

His hopeful expectations, derived from the world of comic romance, are shattered by the very nature of events in the most uncompromising fashion by a stage direction:

> *Enter* GLOUCESTER, *led by an* OLD MAN
> EDGAR: But who comes here?
> My father, poorly led? World, world, O world!
> (IV.i.9–10)

But unlike Kent, Edgar is only temporarily daunted, and he can quickly find a new literary prototype on which to base his conduct, a patient stoicism:

> Men must endure
> Their going hence, even as their coming hither:
> Ripeness is all.
>
> (V.ii.9–10)

Patience is the ultimate value in the world of romance, and Edgar is confident that it has its own reward. We cannot conclusively say whether Edgar's constitutional capacity learned from his father, to whistle in the dark, is ludicrously weak or a moral strength. The Edgars among the critics,[6] still clinging to the literary pattern of romance, believe that Lear dies happy and that by the end things can only change for the better, with Edgar's hopeful vision in control:

> The oldest hath borne most; we that are young
> Shall never see so much nor live so long.
>
> (V.iii.325–6)[7]

Edgar has rarely been right before, but if we choose to believe, he may be right this time.

Even Lear himself clings to a belief in romance conventions, and in this he could be forgiven because in his moving reconciliation with Cordelia he appears to have proof of the existence of some providential order which will return all to the best. If he knew the sources for his own story as we do, he would have even more cause for hope because they all deliver him to happier times by the end.[8] His own preferred scenario for the happy ending is interesting, for it is taken essentially from a passage in Spenser which seems to have been a favorite with Shakespeare since he is to return to it in presenting the retired (or rather, banished) old courtier Belarius in *Cymbeline*. Lear's vision is that having been healed of the mental wounds inflicted by living in the courtly ethos, and having been rejoined by his beloved daughter under such miraculous conditions, he has won the right to be happy, wise, and helpful to others, even in prison:

> Come, let's away to prison.
> We two alone will sing like birds i' th' cage;
> When thou dost ask me blessing, I'll kneel down
> And ask of thee forgiveness; so we'll live,
> And pray, and sing, and tell old tales, and laugh

> At gilded butterflies, and hear poor rogues
> Talk of court news; and we'll talk with them too —
> Who loses and who wins; who's in, who's out —
> And take upon's the mystery of things
> As if we were God's spies; and we'll wear out
> In a wall'd prison packs and sects of great ones
> That ebb and flow by th' moon.
>
> (V.iii.8–19)

Critics who sternly admonish Lear for creating yet another false illusion[9] are being rather uncompassionate, for there is surely little else he can do without simply accepting despair as his only option. He is admitting defeat by worldly forces, but in a way that is faithful to the romance of *Romeo and Juliet*, he is determined to make the best of things. He is no better, no worse, at this point than anybody else in the play since they all live by illusions to some extent, and his own vision of the promised end at least has the virtue of gentle peace. The relevant piece in Spenser holds in it a deep sanity, for it too, in the book concerned with evils of the court, presents a similar vision which has in this instance been realized:

> For whylome he had bene a doughty Knight,
>   As any one, that liued in his daies,
>   And proued oft in many perillous fight,
>   Of which he grace and glory wonne alwaies,
>   And in all battels bore away the baies.
>   But being now attacht with timely age,
>   And weary of this worlds vnquiet waies,
>   He tooke him selfe vnto this Hermitage,
> In which he liu'd alone, like careless bird in cage.
>
> (*The Faerie Queene*, VI.vi.4)

The Hermit provides a still center, full of pastoral peace and healing qualities, in *The Faerie Queene*, and one might detect in his presentation an element of wish-fulfilment on Spenser's part in the rather disillusioned and melancholy Book of Courtesy. That the impulse is a universal one, and more to do with the mind than specific material conditions, finds unexpected proof in the moving and heartfelt finale to Oscar Wilde's *De Profundis*.[10] Lear's vision then, a hopeful one in a hopeless situation, is neither facile nor an index of congenital self-delusion. It is perfectly appropriate, and a blessed mental refuge, discovered by one who feels sure that he is living in a romance world, and again the sources for the play are enough to make the hopefulness a valid supposition. This moment of the play is one of the warming fires that glow occasionally in the play, and the embers come from romance. But, it is argued, by this time Shakespeare himself is troubled by the genre, and by its proximity to a dangerous reliance upon illusions that fly in the face of facts. It is Shakespeare himself, not the conventions of romance or the hopes of individuals, who determines the ending of the play which savagely returns us to the existence of evil, as well as the existence of fickle fortune and disastrous accidents.

In a recent book which takes as its center of interest the final scenes in Shakespeare's tragedies, Walter C. Foreman finds interesting parallels between the endings of *King Lear* and *Antony and Cleopatra*. They are, he says, Shakespeare's "most daring" tragic conclusions in that they both have final scenes "that as far as the plot is concerned are gratuitous".[11] In *King Lear* the "inevitable" conclusion (the reunion of Lear and Cordelia) is avoided by being passed by, and a series of ironic accidents governs the actual ending. In *Antony and Cleopatra* the inevitable ending is delayed so that it may more obviously be seen as "a single character's intentional creation". With the knowledge we have acquired from romance we may be even more specific. In *Lear* each of the characters holds a different expectation of what is the "inevitable" ending, ranging from love-romance, chivalric revenge, through to pure comedy where disguises will be shed and social reunion will be enacted in an *ensemble* scene. For Albany, who harps often upon the notion of poetic justice, the ending will bring about a just apportionment of praise for the virtuous and blame for the evil. What in fact happens, when Lear brings on the body of Cordelia, amounts to a shattering of all these expectations which have been formulated according to literary paradigms. The strong implication is that literature is not adequate for understanding or explaining accidents and evil. The play reflects further on Shakespeare's disillusionment with romance in particular and all optimistic literary artifices in general. However, there are enough flames flickering at certain points in the play to show that the dramatist is no longer so dismissive as he had been in *Troilus and Cressida* of the values lying beneath romance, such as love, friendship, and hope. Edgar's repeated "Look up" may not be enough to avert disaster, but at least it provides a way of coping, a means for the living to continue even after the greatest misery has occurred. Enough of the romance vision is left intact for Shakespeare to draw upon, and indeed, judging from the plays that follow, *King Lear* has somehow enabled him to turn some corner.

To quote Foreman again, he suggests that *Antony and Cleopatra* "extends tragic form by bringing comic rhythm into a tragic structure", by allowing Cleopatra to orchestrate her own death scene in a way that gives her victory rather than defeat. Although such a statement is true in its terms, Foreman has limited his categories too rigidly for the play does not simply encapsulate a "comic" principle within a "tragic structure". Rather, Shakespeare gives us a play which has an unusually heightened concentration upon death itself, viewed from a vantage point offered by romance. This is to give a much more complex gloss than that implied in Susanne Langer's statement from which Foreman takes his lead: "The matrix of the [dramatic] work is always either tragic or comic; but within its frame the two often interplay."[12]

It is one of the unique and often neglected qualities of this work that Antony and Cleopatra talk more about death than any other tragic hero except Hamlet, and right from the beginning their imagery is full of dying. Whereas for other tragic heroes death comes accidentally or suddenly after they have spent the whole play trying to resist it, here the central characters are preparing themselves quite consciously throughout for their final end. The strategy they use consistently is to make death acceptable and even welcome and beautiful by creating various metaphors to explain its occurrence. Cleopatra has much celerity in dying metaphorically, and Antony can see death first as the relinquishment of service "I look on you As one that takes his leave" (IV.ii.24–9) or as another love affair:

> But I will be
> A bridegroom in my death, and run into't
> As to a lover's bed. Come then.
>
> IV.xii.99–101)

Cleopatra, so addicted to life and sensual vitality, strives even more strenuously to turn death into something which can be accommodated in the act of living:

> Then is it sin,
> To rush into the secret house of death,
> Ere death come to us?
>
> (IV.xiii.87)

Like Antony, she likens death to love:

> The stroke of death is as a lover's pinch
> Which hurts, and is desir'd.
>
> (V.ii.293–4)

The greater the poetic and metaphorical eloquence which she can muster, and the closer she can bring death into the orbit of her desire to be alive, the more decisive becomes Cleopatra's attitude until she persuades herself (and a receptive audience) that the categories are reversed, that dying is living, whereas under conditions of humiliation living can be death. The powerful effect of the deaths of these mature lovers is generated because they cannot fall back on any given external code or given ethic. "The high Roman fashion" is not wholly congenial to people who have discovered that Rome is the enemy to life in its most vibrant sense: the nobleness of life is to do otherwise than the Romans. Moreover, in the pagan world there can be no possibility of Christian consolation. Energetically involved in the joy of living which is so difficult to relinquish, these characters must create their own personal myths in order to accept death. Neither is by temperament philosophically inclined, and their impulse is to act rather than to reflect. The only materials they have to create an attitude to death come from the variousness of images and feelings surrounding them in life. They must use their senses, they must use figurative language and the imagination which is at its most convincing in poetic utterance. In a most astonishing way we find ourselves back in the universe of *A Midsummer Night's Dream*, where the imagination can tease us out of thought, and dreams can be far more true and grand than reality.[13]

Antony and Cleopatra in a sense picks up where *All's Well That End's Well* finishes. The play takes further Helena's belief, and that of romance, that what the imagination sees can be turned into a personal truth. When the lovers are together they bicker and misunderstand each other like any domestic partners, but when they are separated, especially by the final absence, death, Cleopatra sanctifies Antony with her full-blooded acceptance of a mythic conception of him that makes even the most naive romance sentiments seem pale in comparison:

> The crown o'th'earth doth melt. My lord!
> O, wither'd is the garland of the war,
> The soldier's pole is fall'n! Young boys and girls
> Are level now with men. The odds is gone,
> And there is nothing left remarkable
> Beneath the visiting moon.
> (IV.xv.63–8)

To one who can suggest, like Plato in the attack on poets,[14] that such a rhapsody is not truthful, she magnificently turns against him Sidney's defense of the poet's figurative and visionary truth:

> For his bounty,
> There was no winter in't; an autumn 'twas
> That grew the more by reaping. His delights
> Were dolphin-like: they show'd his back above
> The element they liv'd in. In his livery
> Walk'd crowns and crownets; realms and islands were
> As plates dropp'd from his pocket.
> DOLABELLA: Cleopatra —
> CLEOPATRA: Think you were was or might be such a man
>   As this I dreamt of?
> DOLABELLA: Gentle madam, no.

CLEOPATRA: You lie, up to the hearing of the gods.
          But if there be nor ever were one such,
          It's past the size of dreaming. Nature wants stuff
          To vie strange forms with fancy; yet t'imagine
          An Antony were nature's piece 'gainst fancy,
          Condemning shadows quite.

                                        (V.ii.86–100)

The passage recalls many contemporary statements from romance and romantic comedy in its vindication of the dream as reality and its assertion of the improbable products of "fancy" as sublimely valid even when judged against the pragmatic facts of "nature". For example, Sidney writes in this way of the supremacy of the imagination:

> Nature never set forth the earth in so rich tapestry as divers poets have done; neither with so pleasant rivers, fruitful trees, sweet-smelling flowers, nor whatsoever else may make the too much loved earth more lovely. Her world is brazen, the poets only deliver a golden.[15]

The Iago-like, sardonic viewer (or the literal-minded, professionally "truthful" critic) would point out that we should not be taken in by a piece of rhetorical conjuring which leads us to deny the evidence of our own eyes. Antony has in the play been far from a confident, magnificent hero, and some would have us believe that Cleopatra is a dishonest whore. But the fact that this contrary view is often put once again proves the point that the evidence of facts is in itself neutral, and that the interpretations of the imagination at least have the attraction of bestowing a generous value even upon the final, neutral fact, death. The interior message of romance, taught by Petruchio,[16] Rosalind, Helena, and the writer of A Midsummer Night's Dream, that "even with a thought" reality may be transformed is here used to redeem a waste of time, the relative failure of a love relationship and the martial failures of a man of war. The victory is all the greater in that romance attitudes are tested by mature, middle-aged characters in a world that has the presence of death instead of by young lovers in a world that must culminate in marriage. Wilson Knight, his sights set on the last four "romances" of Shakespeare, also senses that Antony and Cleopatra is a great turning point:

The tragic spirit dominating the sombre plays from *Hamlet* and reaching its maximum intensity in *Timon of Athens* finally transmutes itself, as is the nature of such intensity, to a positive; the reversal being expressed crisply in Timon's "nothing brings me all things" (V.i.193). The full statement of this new position is *Antony and Cleopatra*, less a tragedy than a triumphal song, wherein death is no longer gloomy but golden. The truth revealed is, of course, no logical proposition, but simply a dramatic coherence exploited by poetry (especially the poetry of Cleopatra's dream in Act V), and relying mainly on a sharp synchronization of death with love to create a new intensity that may be called, for want of a better phrase, essential life . . .[17]

And for want of a more formal term to describe such a mode of drama, a term less mongrel than "tragi-comedy", we might apply romance, triumphantly resurrected from its grave in *Troilus and Cressida* and reinstated at the center of Shakespeare's art.

In *Antony and Cleopatra*, Shakespeare seems to have regained confidence in the romance vision as something which can invest value even in desperate circumstances, and his last four plays, perhaps with the exception of *The Tempest*, build upon his renewed faith. Before examining these plays, however, we should remind ourselves that the revival of romance is not simply confined to Shakespeare's writings but is a fact of literary history as well. The causes of the renewed interest in dramatized romance cannot be known, although there is a shred of evidence in connection with the specific revival of the apparently clumsy but remarkably popular play, *Mucedorus*, an adaptation of an incident from Sidney's *Arcadia*, that comedy was more to the King's liking than tragedy,[18] and the currency of the colorful and romance-like masque form, directed to the King at the time, adds weight to the hypothesis. Furthermore, many of the plays (including *Mucedorus* itself) were presented at the aristocratic, coterie theatres, which suggests that the once popular form had become rather *chic*, perhaps for its very naivety and its potential for sophisticated audience participation. Be this as it may, it seems that in the years between about 1608 and 1612, romance became popular again on the stage.[19] We have Beaumont and Fletcher's burlesque of the romance, *The Knight of the Burning Pestle*, and the same authors' *Philaster, or Love Lies a-Bleeding* and *A King and No King*, all tragi-comedies owing much to romance conventions. Fletcher's *The Faithful Shepherdess* is a pastoral romance, and several comedies, such as the undistinguished *The Dumb Knight* by Markham and Machin, revive memories of the titles of "lost" plays of the 1570s and 80s. Rowley's *The Birth of Merlin, or the Child Hath Found His Father* declares in its title its romance pedigree. The most characteristic note of the best of these plays, such as Beaumont and Fletcher's, is an enduring theatricality which depends a lot on teasing audience expectations. In a play like *Philaster* we are kept in doubt until the very end about whether the dénouement will be happy or tragic, and one feels that the effect of this is not the creation of a homogeneous, "tragi-comic" tone or vision of life but more like the effect of a detective story where many clues are left which could be *intellectually* unravelled but the audience is kept puzzled until the last.[20] I shall argue that this kind of Jacobean romance, depending on oscillation between emotional involvement and intellectual distancing, is particularly significant for interpreting *Cymbeline*.

Finally, of course, we find the four great plays which will next claim our attention, towards which this book has been building: *Pericles, Cymbeline, The Winter's Tale*, and *The Tempest*. Even with their common use of romance motifs, each of these plays is radically different in nature, and they demonstrate Shakespeare's extraordinary capacity to refresh conventions whenever he wrote. The plays are not primarily comedies which take motifs from literary romance, but instead they are fully accomplished but differing romances in dramatic form. Therefore, our question ceases to be "what do these plays borrow from romance?" Instead, it becomes "in what ways are these plays romances, and what do they contribute to romance itself?"

VI Shakespeare's Romances

Pericles

Pericles is the one and only pure romance in the Shakespearean canon, and viewed as such it has a strange and moving beauty of its own. The courtly wit of the early comedies is replaced by a hushed honesty of poetic statement and a sense of reverent awe, as a man finds himself at the mercy of the elements and the gods. As the play moves through its recurrent rhythms of turbulence and stillness, grief and joy, the central figure can adopt only humble patience as his basic point of view, fully aware that he is involved in living a life which lies at the discretion of destiny:

> We cannot but obey
> The powers above us. Could I rage and roar
> As doth the sea she lies in, yet the end
> Must be as 'tis.
>
> (III.iii.9–12)

A sense of miracle and mystery informs the movement of the story and hangs in the air around the most astonishing mystery of all, the human capacity to remember, so that the past becomes a part of the present.

Shakespeare returns in *Pericles* to the oldest form of narrative romance — not only to its source in Apollonius of Tyre but also to Heliodorus, Achilles Tatius, and the *Odyssey* — and he creates out of these romances of the sea perhaps the one wholly successful dramatized version in English of this essentially episodic and narrative form. Like Spenser, Shakespeare realizes that the sea itself is the element which can bind such stories to an eternal rhythm, and the journey carries Fortune's message instead of simply creating a neat situation for further developments on land as in plays like *The Comedy of Errors, Twelfth Night,* and *The Tempest.* Man is placed at the center, but within an immeasurably large universe of time and destiny, surrounded by all the dangers faced by the mariner in a storm:

As Pilot well expert in perilous waue,
That to a stedfast starre his course hath bent,
When foggy mistes, or cloudy tempests haue
The faithfull light of that faire lampe yblent,
And couer'd heauen with hideous dreriment,
Vpon his card and compas firmes his eye,
The maisters of his long experiment,
And to them does the steddy helme apply,
Bidding his winged vessell fairely forward fly.
                                    (*Faerie Queene*, II.vii.1)

And so does Pericles, helplessly but studiously, navigate his life.

To see *Pericles* as anything less than a near-perfect dramatic romance is to judge its accomplishment by the wrong standards. It is a straightforward revival of a mode extremely popular in the 1580s, and a revival which succeeds where they failed. Eyewitness accounts of narrative romance placed on the stage during the earlier period are unsympathetic, and the reason seems to be that the plays lacked the true heartbeat of feeling and inwardness with romance as a way of looking at the world which *Pericles* achieves so triumphantly. Sidney's description of the staged romances which he had seen asserts that romantic drama is inferior to Italian comedy as a dramatic form, if indeed romance is a form at all. He condemns the plays for not obeying the Aristotelian unities, and for requiring us to make impossible assumptions about the time and places represented on the stage "which, how absurd it is in sense, even sense may imagine, and art hath taught, and all ancient examples justified — and at this day, the ordinary players in Italy will not err in."[1] His dismissive description of a typical play implies that the early plays took over wholesale the plots of romance — travel to far-flung regions, desultory battles, life stories of knights, their ladies and children — but without a convincing and central point of view. George Whetstone launched a similar attack, condemning the English playwright because he "groundes his works on impossibilities",[2] flouting credibility and ignoring the dramatic unities. His description suggests, but does not condone, a positive kind of drama, based on love, separation, travel, quests, reversals of fortune, and spectacle, but the plays fail for lack of quality ("indiscrete workinge") and lack of theatrical effectiveness. Stephen Gosson attacks the romantic plays chiefly on the grounds that they are not concerned with teaching virtue. "What learne you by that?"[3] he demands, after describing the kind of rambling narrative mentioned by Sidney and Whetstone. With this inauspicious pedigree, Shakespeare saw fit at the time of his greatest maturity to turn back to dramatic romance. Without the elegant self-sufficiency of the love plot in a romantic comedy, and without the hints of self-parody of *Cymbeline*, and without the complex mixture of modes adopted in *The Winter's Tale* and *The Tempest*, *Pericles* is pure dramatized romance, and as such should be evaluated and understood in its own terms. However disputed is the question of particular sources,[4] there is no doubt that they lie in the region of narrative romance pure and simple, without irony or allegory, and for this reason also the play should be judged in terms of the genre itself and the limits which it sets for itself. The Greek and medieval story of Apollonius of Tyre and the conventional bed of adventures encountered by Sidney's Pyrocles come from an ancient and solemn stock going right back to the *Odyssey*, a mode that presents time and eternity, men and gods, birth and death, along a single line of consciousness. Whetstone's rhetorical question, "What learne you by that?" can be answered after the experience of *Pericles*: we learn the largest lessons, that patience in adversity is a supreme virtue, that despair is a sin, and that using the human capacities for memory and hope, time and nature will arrange eventually for good to assert itself over the forces of evil and of fortuitous calamity. The moral categories of romance are large, but that is because eternity is large. The triumph of romance morality is the triumph of endless time over circumstance and over endings.

Commentators agree, with some minor quibbles, that Shakespeare took over another dramatist's play at the beginning of Act III.[5] By common consent what he immediately begins to add to the play is dramatic poetry of an immeasurably higher quality. He may find different centers of interest — in particular, familial relationships rather than courtly intrigue — but he does not radically alter the direction of generic expectations. The play has already asserted itself as a romance with its anonymous, virtuous knight confronting forces of evil, its pageantry, its large scale of time and space, its rudimentary moral categories, and its narrative basis, resting on reconciliation and separation. If the play had continued at the same tempo and the same measure of poetic relaxation it would have been little better, and no worse, than the dramatized romances deplored by earlier critics — plays such as *Clyomon and Clamydes* and *Common Conditions*. Of course, the sudden shift of gear in poetic concentration and intensity is part of the process of lifting the play into a higher realm, but in addition, and perhaps more important, Shakespeare begins to *generalize* the experience. He immediately declares himself to be in control of the medium rather than at its mercy, consciously working in the furrows of ancient romance but genuinely adapting it to a new mode of drama, rather than simply assuming that the narrative itself will work its effect as it does in the ample, sprawling works of prose romance. He knows he is painting a very large picture on a small canvas, and accordingly he adapts his materials and his instruments. He does this in two ways. First, the scene where he picks up the story is deliberately placed on a scale and a plane that takes the narrative itself into vast reaches of time, space, and morality to declare its largest significance. Secondly, he uses the figure of Gower, who has probably been given to him by the innovatory craftsmanship of his collaborator, to achieve more ambitious ends than simply those of a narrator in a prose work who can tide us over inessential parts of the plot.

III.i spans the spectrum of artistic representation from an intense realization of the sounds and sights of the stormy night at sea through to the rarest of mystical experiences, an apprehension of how inseparably involved are the processes of being born, of living, and of dying. The scene begins with an invocation of gods who determine not only the moral life but the elements:

> Thou god of this great vast, rebuke these surges,
> Which wash both heaven and hell, and thou that hast
> Upon the winds command, bind them in brass,
> Having call'd them from the deep! O, still
> Thy deaf'ning, dreadful thunders; gently quench
> Thy nimble sulphurous flashes!

(III.i.1–6)

Images are both specific and numinous, describing noise, and at the same time placing humanity in an insignificant corner of the universe:

> The seaman's whistle
> Is as a whisper in the ears of death,
> Unheard.
>
> (III.i.8–10)

At this moment the child is placed in the hands of Pericles, a "piece" of his dead queen and born at the moment of her death out of the very shudder and pangs of the heaving storm:

> Now, mild may be thy life!
> For a more blusterous birth had never babe;
> Quiet and gentle thy conditions! for
> Thou art the rudeliest welcome to this world
> That ever was prince's child. Happy what follows!
> Thou hast as chiding a nativity
> As fire, air, water, earth, and heaven, can make,
> To herald thee from the womb.
>
> (III.i.26–34)

Superstition may express a symbolic truth, and the sailors insist that in order to still the storm the body of the wife must be given to the sea, for nature cannot tolerate the non-living. She will go, however, to the stillness at the center of existence which dimly we intuit to be the genesis as well as the exodus of creation:

> A terrible childbed hast thou had, my dear;
> No light, no fire. Th'unfriendly elements
> Forgot thee utterly; nor have I time
> To give thee hallow'd to thy grave, but straight
> Must cast thee, scarcely coffin'd, in the ooze;
> Where, for a momument upon thy bones,
> And aye-remaining lamps, the belching whale
> And humming water must o'erwhelm thy corpse,
> Lying with simple shells.
>
> (III.i.56–64)

In this one scene, Shakespeare has spanned extremes of time and imagination that are essential to the romance experience, especially at the time of the endless ending at its most permanent level where death rolls into birth, grief into action, storm into serenity, for time without ending. When placed within the large scope of the gods and the elements, human life is as insignificant and unheard as a whisper, as precarious as a duck in a storm (III. Chorus, 1. 49). But when apprehended from within as the fact of creation itself, the same human life has a warm miraculousness and sanctity that shadows and overshadows all the rest of the tangible world and the remote gods. The immensity of the sea, identified with destiny and history, is juxtaposed with the warm, tiny baby. Up to this scene, the story has been little better than a good yarn, full of incident and suspense. Now it is suddenly something much larger. The scene is elemental, a storm at sea. The situation is human: a man is confronted with the simplest and most mysterious occurrences of death and birth simultaneously. In this scene, after his many experiments with the human dimensions of romance, Shakespeare has reached its *raison d'être*, and has opened up the philosophy that experience may be apprehended through both ends of a telescope at the same time.

The device of Gower as presenter of the action may be Shakespeare's idea, but it is simpler to assume that it was introduced by the collaborator. It is, in fact, a cleverly functional way of getting around the more obvious problems in adapting a story well-known in prose romance to the foreshortening medium of the drama. Gower replaces the narrator in the prose work, the person who can explain the action, fill in long gaps in time, provide an occasional moral comment on the goodness or wickedness of the characters, establish a friendly, trusting relationship with the audience, and ultimately, by judicious framing of events, allow the episodes of action to speak for themselves. Time and again he insists, like the Chorus in *Henry V*, that the audience must exercise its imagination, in order to accept the changes of time and scene:

> Be attent,
> And time that is so briefly spent
> With your fine fancies quaintly eche:
> (III.Chorus.11–3)

> In your imagination hold
> This stage the ship, upon whose deck
> The sea-toss'd Pericles appears to speak.
> (58–60)
> Imagine Pericles arriv'd at Tyre,
> Welcom'd and settled to his own desire.
> (IV.Chorus.1–2)
> The unborn event
> I do commend to your content;
> Only I carried winged time
> Post on the lame feet of my rhyme;
> Which never could I so convey,
> Unless your thoughts went on my way.
> (45–50)

His intimate tone with the audience creates a moment of friendly sociability at the end when he thanks the audience for their attentiveness, patience, and co-operativeness. Gower is created as the storyteller in Sidney's mode, keeping children from play and old men from the chimney corner with the simplicity and enchantment of his telling. Technically speaking, he turns what could have been a rambling, barely connected sequence of events into a series of tightly constructed and dramatically intense episodes. In his attitude to the story itself, Gower is the narrator well-known in romance, continually referring back to his book, his historical record which he is simply re-telling, and he establishes the agelessness of the tale:

> To sing a song that old was sung,
> From ashes ancient Gower is come,
> Assuming man's infirmities,
> To glad your ear, and please your eyes.
> It hath been sung at festivals,
> On ember eves and holy-ales;
> And lords and ladies in their lives
> Have read it for restoratives.
> (I.Chorus.1–8)

By being "ancient" Gower and self-confessedly "an old man", he places himself in our own world of mortality and aging — the world in which we see Pericles grow old — while pushing the story itself back into an age before time itself, a world transcending time. In his scene-setting he is on the one hand bald and rudimentary in speaking of the story, but precise and evocative in suggesting that we are simultaneously witnessing a scene and also ourselves *part* of a different scene hearing his tale, and at times the two dimensions meet:

> The cat, with eyne of burning coal,
> Now couches 'fore the mouse's hole;
> And crickets sing at the oven's mouth
> Aye the blither for their drouth.
>
> (III.Chorus.5–8)

That word "now" has a reference backwards into an historical present, and a more immediate sense for us, as we sit at the feet of the story-teller. Finally, by mentioning twice the skill of Marina in creating some work of art such as music or needlework, Gower uses Sidney's device from the *Arcadia* in reference to Pamela[6] in order to sharpen the distinctions still further between artifice and reality, time and timelessness, in such a way that each of the dimensions is eternally present in the experience of a living audience witnessing an event which, however fictional and ancient, is living before our eyes. With a disarming simplicity the presence of Gower as a narrator takes the dramatist much of the way toward convincing us that the dénouement contains the true romance sensation of a timeless event which is being enacted in time. The combination of stilted artifice in the lines of Gower and the tonal familiarity in his relationship with the audience causes the story itself, the action, to spill out of its boundaries of convention and improbability, into a set of animated and lifelike events, more or less as the time-bound contours of the play eventually swell into an experience of timeless significance.

At the beginning of the final Act, Pericles and Marina, father and daughter, are both revealed in a pose as static as art. Pericles has immobilized himself, having not spoken for three months, and he is "discovered", presumably behind a curtain, like a statue. Marina, with her "sweet harmony" likened often to a goddess, exists at this moment also as a cameo, framed in a leafy shelter on the edge of the island. Her physic is music, an art that moves through time and yet plays on stillness, and she has the equal permanence and impermeability of an allegory of a living statue:

> for thou lookest
> Modest as Justice, and thou seem'st a palace
> For the crown'd Truth to dwell in.
> . . .
>   Yet thou dost look
> Like Patience gazing on kings' graves, and smiling
> Extremity out of act.
>   (V.i.119–39 *passim*)

It is extraordinarily apt and moving that in this image Shakespeare is harking back some eight years in his own creative life to Viola who sat like patience on a monument, for the immobilizing element at work in these two characters is the sad loss of a past which must now lovingly be retrieved and re-connected.[7] Pericles' story is "too tedious to repeat", and it springs from the loss of a beloved daughter and a wife, an estrangement from the only tangible relics that could prove the existence of his own long and stressful existence on earth. Equally, Marina was once highborn, but nothing remains of her past:

> My derivation was from ancestors
> Who stood equivalent with mighty kings;
> But time hath rooted out my parentage,
> And to the world and awkward casualties
> Bound me in servitude.
>   (V.i.89–93)

She confesses her own discarded past, a present truth which can always be told of things that are no more:

> If I should tell my history, it would seem
> Like lies, disdain'd in the reporting.
>   (V.i.117–8)

The managerial fussiness, the executive prying, of the petty people around who have no past themselves of consequence to this event, enhances, and does not distract from the stillness between two people who slowly, like sleepwalkers, realize that filaments to the truth of a personal past are beginning to glow.

For Lysimachus there is "sacred physic" (V.i.73) in the reconciliation, and for Pericles, as he lovingly runs the fingers of
his mind around the beauty of Marina, and around the loosely
bound, refound relationship with his daughter, the event is the
sign that sleeping existence has joined the waking so fluently
that his own past is his present, and there is no rift of separ-
ateness:

> O, stop there a little!
> This is the rarest dream that e'er dull sleep
> Did mock sad fools withal. This cannot be:
> My daughter's buried. Well, where were you bred?
> I'll hear you more, to th' bottom of your story,
> And never interrupt you.
>
> (V.i.159–64)

Surely the greatest mystery is how the things that are no more,
that we call simply "memory" or stories, are still now, and still
with us as a part of what the present is. Now the hero of the
play may declare his identity, and be liberated into present
existence, his history validated and reintegrated:

> I am Pericles of Tyre; but tell me now
> My drown'd queen's name, as in the rest you said
> Thou hast been godlike perfect,
> The heir of kingdoms and another life
> To Pericles thy father.
>
> (V.i.203–7)

And Marina can slip in the final detail to prove that she is no
goddess but a human being with her own past that connects
with the existence of others:

> Is it no more to be your daughter than
> To say my mother's name was Thaisa?
> Thaisa was my mother, who did end
> The minute I began.
>
> (V.i.208–10)

The genius of Shakespeare lies in his capacity to give the
simplest words to the strangest capillaries of the flowing blood
of living people in the extremity of feeling. With the music of
the spheres he goes on to remind us that the moment is a

sacred awakening whose occurrence coaxes us to believe in miracles and in the existence of gods. And at this moment there is indeed a goddess on hand to remind Pericles that he must draw the sleeping and the waking parts of his mind into a clear conjunction, or else he will be condemned to a split between his own past and his future. Diana appears, and speaks:

> Reveal how thou at sea didst lose thy wife.
> To mourn thy crosses, with thy daughter's, call,
> And give them repetition to the life.
> Or perform my bidding or thou liv'st in woe;
> Do it, and happy — by my silver bow!
> Awake, and tell thy dream.
>
> (V.i.242-7)

The play has awakened a deity at this moment specifically in order to prove that gods and goddesses do not exist except for human uses. The supernatural is an explanation, a justification, a reminder of the most moving and significant human recognitions, people reunited with their individual pasts and with the collective, fragmented pasts of others.

All within this scene has been within human comprehension, a wonderful but not impossible accident of meeting whose significance is to rejoin not only a father and a daughter but two personal versions of the past to a verifiable present. What remains in the short, final scene is to complete the story in a fictively satisfying manner, to reconcile Pericles and his daughter with the most notionally important person of all, a wife and a mother. Perhaps it is fictional only, and improbable when judged by the narrowest standards of probability that Thaisa lives as Diana's nun and can be reconciled with her husband and daughter. But since we have witnessed, within the sphere of the possible, events that may easily be ascribed to the supernatural, Shakespeare is prepared here to take the gamble and trust that our faith here has been so awakened to the *potential* beauty of the rhythms that life has given us — separation and reunion — that we may be convinced of this final device of his plot. Once we accept the miracles of history and of the way the timeless memory may occasionally determine events within time, then little lies in our way to project our imaginations into the hypothetical wonder of living a life and yet knowing that every moment is a moment of full existence in which everything from the past may unexpectedly be called into being as a part of the living present.

It is necessary to make a narrow but significant distinction concerning the kind of reconciliation effected at the end of *Pericles*. It is not so important, as it is at the end of *The Winter's Tale*, that a *family* has been brought together again. It is more accurate to say that each individual has been brought into living relationship again with his or her own past, and that in a strangely haunting way this leaves each still in some sense alone, and separate. Each individual has had to live in full, again, the traces of his or her past: such a redefinition of personal identity, such a refocussing of "now", brings on absorbed reflections in self. A space for solitude still surrounds each character, even in community. After all, Pericles, Marina, and Thaisa have never really had time to know each other, even in pairs. The feeling that permeates the ending is significantly different in *The Winter's Tale* where the dramatic attention is placed upon the reconciliation between a husband and wife who had, before the rupture, lived closely with each other for several years. Perdita is somewhat an outsider to this warm and joyous event, and her presence at court has more of a symbolic value in providing the occasion for a true family reconciliation. *Pericles* dwells more on the notion of continuity re-established in the personal history of separate individuals. For Pericles, Marina *is* Thaisa as she was when his young wife, while for Leontes, Hermione is herself, and has lived for as long as he has. Leontes picks up the threads in the present, within time: Pericles is allowed to go back in time and pick up the threads from the occasion of the storm. At the endings of both plays there is a sense of regret at *temps perdu*, but the feeling operates in different ways.[8]

It is worth adding that, although Shakespeare may have taken over the writing of *Pericles* from an inferior dramatist, he manages to make the play into a unity by concentrating upon the substance of the fragment he uses. The idea that the play represents a man retrieving his personal past is built into even the first two Acts. Pericles is specific on the point that he is losing touch with his own past as he goes from country to

country shedding relationships, status, and even identity,
until he becomes simply an anonymous knight from the romance world. When he is washed up on the shore of
Pentapolis, he says to the courteous and generous Fishermen:

> What I have been I have forgot to know;
> But what I am want teaches me to think on:
> A man thronged up with cold.
>
> (II.i.71–3)

Then, when he meets the kind old king Simonides, the father
of his future wife, he is stirred to recall something of the past
he has lost, and to reflect upon the occurrence:

> Yon king's to me like to my father's picture,
> Which tells me in that glory once he was;
> Had princes sit like stars, about his throne,
> And he the sun, for them to reverence;
>   . . .
> Where now his son's like a glowworm in the night,
> The which hath fire in darkness, none in light.
> Whereby I see that Time's the king of men;
> He's both their parent, and he is their grave,
> And gives them what he will, not what they crave.
>
> (II.iii.36–48)

Shakespeare raises such casual asides to the status of large
statements on human existence by building into his fable the
notion of a person, through familial reconciliation, discovering
something of his own lost past. Even the most sensational
incident, the initial incest between the King of Antioch and
his daughter, is curiously reversed and seen through a glass
darkly by Shakespeare, when he draws the greatest warmth
out of the reconciliation of Pericles and his own daughter:

> I am great with woe, and shall deliver weeping.
> My dearest wife was like this maid, and such a one
> My daughter might have been.
>
> (V.i.105–7)

With a trembling tenderness that could never be demeaned by
the use of the word "incest", Pericles shows how human and
reasonable it may be for an elderly man to see in his daughter

the image of a wife whom he loved as a young woman and whom he lost while she was still young:

> My queen's square brows;
> Her stature to an inch; as wand-like straight;
> As silver-voic'd; her eyes as jewel-like,
> And cas'd as richly; in pace another Juno;
> Who starves the ears she feeds, and makes them hungry
> The more she gives them speech.
>
> (V.i.107–12)

His daughter at this moment is cased as richly as a work of art, yet she is warmly human, "mortally brought forth", and her presence is like a memory which is re-created in the present. Of course, Shakespeare is doing nothing so crudely schematic as to suggest a repetition of the feelings of the King of Antioch, but in the early *datum* of the play he has found a significance that can be brought back unobtrusively so that the play's own past may be mirrored, with profound differences, and the present may be seen as repetition dressed with the glow of an eternal present. Living memory is the fulcrum around which the play turns, and the deepest re-membrance of all is that of the storm at the center which even the grownup Marina, in some curious way (IV.i.54ff.), can remember in detail, having been told so often by her nurse. The sea which takes away and destroys also acts as a magical preservative, and can bring back in its tides until it seems like the capacity for human memory itself.

In an unobtrusive moment Marina, too, is reconciled with her own past, for she is given in marriage to Lysimachus, the main customer at the brothel in which she had stayed, and a man whom she had converted to a purer way of life. In this liaison, we might be tempted to see Shakespeare's charac-teristically sardonic or perfunctory teaming-up of available partners in order to manipulate a wholly neat ending. How-ever, here there seems to be a more intrinsic aptness. Whereas Pericles had initially run away from the apprehension of evil in the court of Antioch, feeling slightly tainted himself by its presence, Marina in the brothel was as militantly virtuous and evangelical as Britomart, Spenser's figure of chastity. Re-fusing to run away or to compromise, Marina has stoically refused to recognize any personal implication in the evil around her, but instead has sought to convert it into virtue. She cannot hope to succeed with the professionals in the brothel since, as the Bawd pertinently and rather touchingly points out, society will not allow them the luxury of being respectable — they must shift for themselves as best they may, or else undertake even more degrading and potentially damaging occupations, such as going into the army in order to lose a leg (like Ralph in *The Shoemaker's Holiday*). With Lysimachus it is otherwise. Nobly born, he has a full choice over whether to conduct a life of good or evil, and under Marina's influence he chooses good. It would not be appropriate for Pericles to be reminded of the court of Antioch since he himself had willingly chosen to forsake this part of his own personal history (and we discover, accordingly, that the King of Antioch is dead). But for Marina, if she is to be reunited with her own past, it is essential that the brothel interlude be recalled and absorbed into her life in the present since she had not flinched from it, and at the time she had accepted responsibility for changing it. We should not make too much of her betrothal at the end, since primarily it is a convenience to round off the story, but there is certainly a deeper appropriateness in it than immediately strikes the eye, and the episode fits into the vision of the play as a whole.

Pericles is a play that majestically invites complete dismissal by the mind which strives to work in a purely rational way by its own utter submission to a naked sense of the wonder of life lived through time. Because it is so loftily uncompromising to scepticism and niggling doubts, it is not only a true romance but it is also not particularly popular,[9] since we always presume that Shakespeare is, if nothing else, rational. I hope to have shown that the fault lies in us, not in the play. There are enough hints in the worldly-wise words of Gower to reassure us that Shakespeare is still himself, cautiously guarding himself against the most ungenerous and mean-minded of "rationalists" by conceding that his story is merely a story, and nothing else. He had done the same many years earlier in the words of a self-proclaimed fairy, Puck, at the end of *The Midsummer Night's Dream*, and there still seems enough in that play to enchant and disturb audiences. "The truest poetry is the most feigning" said one of his most corrosively cynical creations, Touchstone, and although Shakespeare is the most elusive of writers, hedging himself with the intelligent camouflage of rationalism, it may be true that occasionally we can take his words straight as an expression of a born storyteller who is also trying to tell the truth.

Cymbeline

Cymbeline can be claimed as a successful and charming dramatized romance, lightened by an impish mingling of modes at some points, relaxed and ample in its spread of characters, settings, and incidents. It lacks the sacramental solemnity and metaphysical ambition of *Pericles* — which is to say that I remain unconvinced by Wilson Knight's larger claims[10] — but instead there is a golden charm in the way that fairy story often meets practical demands in the action. At some points, Shakespeare seems to have enhanced, rather than explained away, the intrinsic improbabilities in his romance material, but not to the extent that the play can be seen as in any way a sustained parody. There is an air of indulgent enjoyment and continuous theatrical effectiveness which makes *Cymbeline* attractive and relatively undemanding, and it would be only with some awkwardness and at the expense of the good humor for us to make claims for profundity of thought. Here, perhaps, Shakespeare exploits another central characteristic of romance in the occasion it gives for sheer, richly colored enjoyment. He flexes his poetic muscles a couple of times, creating the wonderfully hushed and aesthetically compelling scene in which Iachimo watches the sleeping Imogen and the beautiful mix of rustic geniality and flower poetry in the pastoral scenes, but by and large the play is not concentrated in its poetic texture.

The final Act has usually been seen as the least inspiring. It is rather late in the day to return to earlier critical views that it was not written by Shakespeare,[11] since there is no special reason for suggesting this. We can, however, judge the final Act as a thoroughly competent theatrical solution to the various problems of resolving very disparate materials, leaving the audience with a sense of satisfying completeness and amiable entertainment. The fact that there are half a dozen other contemporaries who were quite capable of writing the poetry is not sufficient for us to say that Shakespeare laid down his pen at the end of Act IV, and like a Renaissance master in an academy of art left an apprentice to finish it off. We can instead say that here Shakespeare is displaying a journeyman's accomplishment, satisfying the requirements of his audience and his material in a most expert, if not virtuoso, way. For once, his astonishing capacity for economy is not on show.

The point concerning the general efficiency of the ending is quite neatly made by a glance at the tonal inappropriateness of a modern attempt to improve upon it. George Bernard Shaw attempts to make the dénouement more economical in *Cymbeline Refinished*. C. B. Young's description and comment is helpful:

> Cuts and abridgements reduce this to a single scene of some 280 lines where Shakespeare's last scene alone runs to over 480. The gaol scenes and vision are omitted; Scene i, with a single line altered to put the battle in the past, follows a new opening in which a Roman captain tells Philario of their defeat; this merges into a short encounter of Posthumus with Jachimo, and then the final dénouement. The remodelling certainly achieved a neater, less drawn-out ending; but it involved a violent change of tone from the fairy-tale and romantic atmosphere of the earlier acts to the Shavian wit, with a touch of cynicism, of the end. Shaw's reputation and the unfamiliarity of theatre audiences with the original doubtless carried off the incongruity.[12]

In such a leisurely and gently amusing play as *Cymbeline*, the original presentation of the ending has function, although we might agree that Shaw's rewriting (as well as his pungent comments on the play in general) helps to focus the problems which modern audiences, somewhat out of touch with the tone of Elizabethan romance, may find in the original.

Since the last Act of the play presents an orderly, perhaps schematic, sequence of resolutions, I might be forgiven for attempting the same in analysis. In turn, we shall look at some of the characters whom the dramatist brings together at the end, and in order to appreciate the well-rounded neatness (and to understand how some measure of vitality has been deliberately forfeited in the interests of presenting an overall pattern), we can glance back to see the problems which have been solved. In this enterprise, it is useful to discriminate two general groups of characters; (1) Imogen, Posthumus, and Iachimo, who earlier in the play had threatened to overspill their function and become interestingly complex in their own right. These characters are uniformly flattened into the service of their role at the end. (2) Other characters who throughout have served the purposes of a convention in romance and are now accepted as having a rightful place of equality in the climax: Cymbeline, Pisanio, Bellarius, and his sons, and the absent but obviously significant villains — the Queen and her son Cloten. Finally, we will glance briefly at the function of the supernatural in bringing about the resolution.

If the dramatist had given to Imogen, Posthumus, and Iachimo in the final Act the freedom to develop their separate characters which he had extended to them in the earlier action, their presence would have destroyed the possibility of achieving the naive romance dénouement. Imogen has been too practical, Posthumus too morally dubious, Iachimo too amorally imaginative, for them acquiescently to fill the rôles demanded of them. Therefore, they need to be put back into a box labelled "romance puppets" in order to let the scheme work itself through unhindered. This necessity does not actually subvert the whole enterprise of the play because their freedom to move has been presented as a charitable concession by the plot which is likely to be withdrawn when the plot itself needs to take priority. What happens is surprisingly similar to the pattern of *Measure for Measure* but with a profound difference of tone. Throughout *Cymbeline*, the air of indulgent good humor operates as a part of the play's vision, and also from the outset the play has announced itself more blatantly as a romance with its boldly diagrammatic presentation of "good" and "evil," leaving us in little doubt that good will triumph over intrigue. A highborn, beautiful lady secretly marries a lowborn but gallant soldier, saving herself from marriage to a universally loathed courtier; but the couple

finds itself under the false protection of a stepmother who is
known to practice "dissembling courtesy" (I.i.85). All this is
known to the audience in the first few minutes of the play, and
it is clearly the stuff of folk tales. Given such an archetypally
clear opening, the dramatist can afford to feel safe within the
generic direction of his tale to spread out his interests a little
into character, knowing that all the threads can be
reassembled and tied together by the end. The comparison
with *Measure for Measure* is interesting since it shows that
Shakespeare could actually base a story on Boccaccio and yet
not make it into a disturbing moral exercise set in a tale of dark
intrigue.

Imogen states her folk tale predicament early in the play:

> A father cruel and a step-dame false;
> A foolish suitor to a wedded lady
> That hath her husband banish'd.
> (I.vi.1–3)

The liberation granted her by the dramatist's licence is to
develop her own character away from the stereotyped romantic
heroine towards a highly practical and at times housewifely
figure. Much of the innocent comedy comes when she finds
herself, in some bewilderment, at odds with the improbabilities of the plot. For example, when taking positive action
to ride to Milford haven, she shows careful attention to the
details of mileage and time, laying a false trail for others by
feigning sickness, and bidding Pisanio to provide her with a
sensible riding-suit "no costlier than would fit/A franklin's
housewife" (III.ii.75–6). But she finds herself plunged into a
strange tale from Pisanio that he has been ordered to kill her,
and she is aided by the luckily benevolent agent when he
produces from his handy bag the various props used in a
romance to disguise the intrepid heroine (III.iv.166ff). The
most famous and much discussed example of the discrepancy
between pragmatism and romance comes when Imogen finds
the dead Cloten and, after cataloguing the clothes he is
wearing from the feet up, she hysterically declares it to be her
husband (IV.ii.291ff). Her systematic observation and description of detail is at odds with the formularistic rhetoric and
the improbable situation. There are many such examples of

this kind of disjunction in the play — most touchingly in the dirge sung by the pastoral characters over Imogen whom they think dead — but they cannot be seen to overturn the basic romance mode or to raise in the audience profound doubts about the nature of reality. Since the audience is usually in the know (and if not, the joke is even more effective), we build up the impression of being in a very safe world controlled by conventions which are ready to pull their rank if the jokes look like getting out of hand. Good is *too* good, evil *too* evil, for us to get particularly worried about the outcome.

However, a direction which could have been genuinely disturbing, if the plot had not called things into line firmly, is the development of character which appears in the presentation of Posthumus and Iachimo. It is perhaps significant that only at the beginning and end (rather changed in both cases) do we see much of these two, because if they had been allowed much more room they could potentially have threatened the dominant spirit. Posthumus, it gradually emerges, is not quite the paragon of all virtues, which is his initial denomination. Through his actions and language he displays a streak of possessiveness over his wife, speaking metaphorically of imprisoning her (I.i.122–3); he is something of a tavern boaster about her fidelity, submits her to a potentially cruel and testing trick which eventually backfires on him, leaps to precipitate conclusions about Imogen's lecherous promiscuity, and reveals a latent sexual resentment because she has withheld her body from him until after marriage. It is Posthumus who speaks the most violently prurient lines, as he fantasizes on his wife's alleged adultery. Even in prison at the end of the play, he shows remarkable hypocrisy in his thinking, assuming that the gods should reward him for his show of penitence after killing Imogen, yet not for a moment considering the possibility that his murder was not just a criminal action, but also a deeply unjust one. Since he still thinks that Imogen was guilty he believes that, however narrowly unlawful his act, it was that of a righteous avenger. In short, he asks the gods for a reward for killing her, and at the same time a reward for showing repentance for killing her. With such a watertight insurance policy, Posthumus is quite sincerely baffled by the apparent absence of swift rewards, and he begins to blame the gods themselves for their injustice.

Whereas Posthumus is potentially a dangerous rogue, held in prison for his own good and the good of the plot until his destructive power is neutralized by good fortune, Iachimo is a rather loveable rogue whose glittering power, almost that of an Edmund, cannot be allowed any free rein after the one scene in which he reveals the damage he could do if liberated. Accordingly, he is banished by the plot at an early stage and reappears at the end as a fully chastened and sadly diminished shadow. Just as he literally pops out of his box in Imogen's bedroom to do some gleeful mischief, so he must firmly be put back into it until he promises to behave himself properly. Iachimo's power derives from his Machiavellian cleverness in goading Posthumus to set up the chastity test on Imogen, but what makes him almost irresistible to the audience is his capacity to speak eloquent poetry:

> The crickets sing, and man's o'erlabour'd sense
> Repairs itself by rest . . .
> . . .
>
>   'Tis her breathing that
> Perfumes the chamber thus. The flame o'th'taper
> Bows toward her and would under-peep her lids
> To see th'enclosed lights, now canopied
> Under these windows white and azure, lac'd
> With blue of heaven's tinct.
>
>   (II.ii.11–23 *passim*)

When he notes Imogen's mole, "cinque-spotted, like the crimson drops/I'th'bottom of a cowslip" (II.ii.38–9), he is recalling Shakespeare's own most fastidiously delicate mode of observation in *A Midsummer Night's Dream*. In the poetic medium of Shakespearean drama, a character who has such eloquent command of his perceptions has a built-in advantage in arresting the audience's attention and inviting its interest. Iachimo even proves himself to be of a finer moral temper than Posthumus when he has a moment of outrage at the thought that anybody should contemplate the kind of trick initiated by Posthumus. Such a notion is never considered by Posthumus himself, who remains self-righteous and vindictive. Iachimo is in love with the sleeping Imogen, and his poetry and moral statements confirm this. When we see him again with Posthumus, however, he is the clever vice- figure, coolly in command of the situation and neatly playing the stops of Posthumus's emotions. Such a versatile, imaginative, and intelligent character as Iachimo is somewhat dangerous to the formularistic categories of romance for it would never do for us to begin to like or admire a man who should be "evil" in the plot. Accordingly, Shakespeare puts him away and forces him to undergo a conversion before he can rejoin the others at the end.

The dramatist, then, creates a certain amount of difficulty for himself by following his instincts for fleshing out characters, since the direction of the developments tends towards making these three people too lively for their roles. The romantic heroine is too pragmatic, the romantic hero is too morally dubious, the villain is too attractive. In passing, however, we might note that such a method is not unprecedented in Elizabethan romance, for Sidney in his *Arcadia* (to which we shall soon return) has gone out of his way to make his characters flawed in order to point towards man's natural degeneracy after original sin, and his ending also flattens the characters back into their designated roles, although in the case of Gynecia he builds into the ending a recognition of her past. In *Cymbeline* the ending is achieved at the expense of the volatile potential in these characters. Imogen, disguised as the serving-boy, speaks mainly in the tones of this role — quietly, unobtrusively, and infrequently. Posthumus's waywardness is forgotten, and he is given the only poetically arresting lines in the whole Act:

> Hang there like fruit my soul,
> Till the tree die.
>
>   (V.v.263)

Admittedly, he strikes Imogen in anger, acting we may feel in character, but his romantic role is gradually retrieved by the amount he is given to say in explanation and in celebration of the happy ending. The reprobate Iachimo is given lines which show a sad change from his earlier eloquence, since he is abject, spiritless, apologetic, and explanatory. By slowing down the pace and spreading thinly the revelations at the end, taking them one by one in orderly fashion, Shakespeare is returning to the ancient spirit of romance, and he is also with great deliberation aligning our interest along the level of plot, forcing us to think of each character as playing an allotted role in the narrative, placing into a receding niche our memories of the lively possibilities in the characters of Imogen, Posthumus, and Iachimo. The memory is left that those moments when they were allowed to show more interesting characteristics (even the striking of Imogen) were primarily exploited for their comedy, rather than upsetting the dominant mode.

If these characters threaten at times to take over the plot with their own unique personalities, they are counterbalanced by others who are more or less completely at the mercy of the plot. Pisanio runs about at the behest of the dramatist, not quite knowing whom he should trust but luckily erring on the side of kindness. He is a quiet, continually compromised character, but like Camillo in *The Winter's Tale* (although showing less knowledge and foresight than Camillo), he steers the plot towards its happy ending, while at the same time being steered himself by "accident" (V.v.278), which in the romance means benevolent providence. He usually acts and speaks out of harrassed fear but in the final Act especially, he is essential to the plot in filling in the missing information for the ensemble. Meanwhile, Bellarius and his two adopted sons are almost straight out of the Spenserian world for they have a boldly allegorical function from which they never escape except at moments when the humor is at their expense, exploiting for comic purposes their own rather slow seriousness. Bellarius, banished from the court wrongly, easily fits into the role of Spenser's hermit in Book VI of *The Faerie Queene*, a rôle which, I have suggested, Lear had aspired to:

> And soothly it was sayd by common fame,
> So long as age enabled him thereto,
> That he had bene a man of mickle name,
> Renowned much in armes and derring doe:
> But being aged now and weary to
> Of warres delight, and worlds contentious toyle,
> The name of knighthood he did disauow,
> And hanging vp his armes and warlike spoyle,
> From all this worlds incombraunce did himselfe assoyle.
>
> (VI.v.37)

Bellarius is the disillusioned knight of courtesy who has chosen the pastoral life quite deliberately while retaining absolute fidelity to his master, the King, even to the extent of bringing up the King's sons. The comedy comes in the inability of the two young men to take his word that they are better off in the country than at court, when they more or less accuse him of living in the past without allowing them to learn for themselves. They mildly mock his wisdom, which sounds to them like platitudinousness. Arviragus and Guiderius are equally Spenserian in their allegorical content, close even to Spenser's "salvage man", who, although uncouth in courtly terms, acts with natural courtesy and, we are assured, was descended from nobility. They are occasionally tricked by the plot, for example, when they think Imogen is dead and speak most beautiful dirges over the body. But the plot can afford to mislead them because they are so schematically there for its benefit, and in the ending it is little more than their presence that is required. Guiderius's moment of rudeness to the King, partly comic in effect, simply reinforces his position as the superficially uncouth but fundamentally noble person:

> GUIDERIUS: Let me end the story:
> I slew him there.
> CYMBELINE: Marry, the gods forfend!
> I would not thy good deeds should from my lips
> Pluck a hard sentence. Prithee, valiant youth,
> Deny't again.
> GUIDERIUS: I have spoke it, and I did it.
> CYMBELINE: He was a prince.
> GUIDERIUS: A most incivil one. The wrongs he did me
> Were nothing prince-like; for he did provoke me
> With language that would make me spurn the sea,
> If it could so roar at me. I cut off's head,
> And am right glad he is not standing here
> To tell this tale of mine.
>
> (V.v.286–97)

Anybody acquainted with Spenser's allegorical strategy would recognize immediately the appropriateness of Guiderius being the executor of Cloten, for the latter is, in the scheme, directly the opposite. He has been boorish and in every way "incivil", relying upon his clothes and appearance to establish his nobility. One could add in this section of characters, that those associated with the war between Rome and Britain perform similarly schematic roles since their presence establishes the final sense of national unity at the end. The unusually large number of these semi-allegorical characters at the end and the gradualness of development as each is used by the plot reinforce the sense that the potentially more lively characters are at this stage being flattened into roles as well, shedding their individuality in order to clarify and advance the unfolding pattern, just as Imogen herself must have layers of disguise and mistaken identities peeled off her in order for the plot to bring order where there was confusion.

Shakespeare is able to contain Iachimo's evil by including amongst his personages a genuinely wicked character, the Queen. She is as close to a stereotyped figure as one could get, and while more typical of the fairy story than the Elizabethan romance (which generally blames Fortune for adversities), she has one literary prototype that Shakespeare would have known well. It is surprising that commentators have not suggested that the Queen is virtually a straight lift from the character of Cecropia in Sidney's *New Arcadia*. Cecropia is the aunt-in-law of the two young heroines, and she is desperately ambitious that her son should marry one of them in order to gain status. Like the Queen, she has an affable front which fools nobody:

> But that sight increased the deadly terror of the princesses, looking for nothing but death since they were in the power of the wicked Cecropia; who yet came unto them, making courtesy the outside of mischief, and desiring them not to be discomforted for they were in a place dedicated to their service.[13]

The Queen is similarly glozing with Imogen:

> No, be assured you shall not find me, daughter,
> After the slander of most stepmothers,
> Evil ey'd unto you. You're my prisoner, but
> Your gaoler shall deliver you the keys
> That lock up your restraint.
>
> (1.i.70–4)

A climax in the *New Arcadia* occurs when Cecropia imprisons the princesses in order to coerce them into marriage. Her son, Amphialus, is a virtuous character, and Cloten bears more resemblance to Cecropia's offsider, Clinias, a coward, a fool, one who has learnt words rather than manners, and one who, having been trained into "a slidingness of language" which has given him vicarious acquaintance with many passions, is capable of cynically using music and song to woo a lady, just as does Cloten (II.iii.10–15).[14] Cecropia eventually encourages her son to rape one of the young women, and later still she tortures Pyrocles with the image of the severed head of his beloved Philoclea.[15] Cecropia shares with the Queen in *Cymbeline* a similarly conscience-stricken and unlamented death at the hands of her own son:

> But when she saw him come in with a sword drawn, and a look more terrible than the sword, she straight was stricken with the guiltiness of her own conscience . . . when she confessed (with most desperate but not repenting mind) the purpose she had to empoison the princesses, and would then have had them murthered. But everybody, seeing, and glad to see her end, had left obedience to her tyranny.[16]

All the significant aspects of the Queen's character and history are paralleled in Sidney's Cecropia, and we can find more supporting evidence that Shakespeare is drawing upon a knowledge of this character from one of the most famous books of the day. He is not just depicting a stock motif from fairy tale, but a familiar and specific literary character, without doing anything to humanize her. His contemporary audience would have been in no doubts about the Queen's unredeemable blackness of heart, and her death would have been fully expected from the outset. Shakespeare uses the report of her death in the last scene also for the purposes of clearing Cymbeline himself of all blame, instating him as a virtuous but honestly misled ruler. Cloten, too, would have been recognized as a type of Clinias who has a penchant for braggardism and involving himself in fights where a coward meets a coward. Cloten's death, too, is recognizably a literary pattern, and Shakespeare portrays it with some comedy. The moment when Imogen thinks his body to be that of Posthumus is also curiously similar to the moment when Cecropia tricks Pyrocles into believing he is looking at the severed head of Philoclea, and again the audience would have recognized a familiar literary situation which can therefore be regarded as not only safely contained in a formula but also mildly comic. In his presentation of the Queen, then, and particularly with the description of her death which clinches the parallel with Cecropia, Shakespeare neatly gives himself the benefit of certain audience expectations derived from contemporary reading which are fulfilled in the last Act.

The slow flamingo dance of recognitions and revelations in the final Act revolves around the figure of Cymbeline himself. He fulfils the function of the Duke-figure in romance, although he is rarely implicated himself. Patiently, judiciously, and rather passively he orchestrates the presentation of the evidence, and his comments generalize and elicit explanations, just as the dukes in conventional romances act. By placing him at the center the dramatist emphasizes the restored harmony of the ending: on a political level, since Britain and Rome are drawn together in amity; on the moral level, since he is himself awakened to his former Queen's treachery; and even metaphysically, since his final image leaves us with the feeling that the links between the moral world and the supernatural forces above are intangible, yet as homely as smoke from a winter chimney:

> Laud we the gods;
> And let our crooked smokes climb to their nostrils
> From our bless'd altars. Publish we this peace
> To all our subjects.
>
> (V.v.475–7)

Again, as in *Pericles*, the gods themselves do not *do* a lot in furthering the action, but the effect of their intrusion is rather different in this play. Whereas in *Pericles* the arrival of Diana enhances the sense of miracle that operates in the mortal world itself since she more or less admits her own ineffectuality unless Pericles himself should want to do something, in *Cymbeline* the supernatural dream and the appearance of Jupiter act in quite a different way. Jupiter represents an avenging moral order which is quick to reprove the errors and inadequacies of lower orders. He even impatiently dismisses the ghosts of mortals for their attempt to intervene, saying that it is for a higher power to patch up the problems:

> Poor shadows of Elysium, hence, and rest
>   Upon your never-withering banks of flow'rs.
> Be not with mortal accidents opprest;
>   No care of yours it is; you know 'tis ours.
>
>   (V.iv.97–100)

Thematically, one might say that the play is here reversing the idea in *Pericles* that a man may be reconciled with his own past, even the dead past, and here the characters are being explicitly cut off from their past in order to arrive at reconciliation. Dramaturgically, the moment of Jupiter's intervention marks the point where the controlling hand of plot and narrative takes over from other concerns such as interest in character. The little scene represents the playwright's advice to us that we are to expect an ending imposed from above, rather than springing wholly naturally from events within the world of "mortal accidents". He is deliberately emphasizing the operation of poetic providence which is characteristic of the older romance ending. But the dramatist cannot resist yet another touch of comic exploitation before he himself gives in to the dictates of plot. The graveyard humor of the Gaoler, full of ghoulish jokes about death, sends up mildly even the king of heaven's lofty omniscience. His earth-bound attitudes make Jupiter's impatient decrees somewhat ridiculous in the context. But even the whimsy of this unexpected character is rapidly despatched in favor of the solemnity of the ensemble of puppets brought on to conclude the play, satisfying the higher priorities of audience expectations and the dramatist's necessity. Nowhere else does Shakespeare quite so nakedly regard his ending as an artefact, drawing attention to the problems he is solving so competently. The effect, however, is not as upsetting as in *Measure for Measure*. It is quite in character for a romantic story which rarely pretends to be anything else. The fact that the soothsayer, the voice of destiny, has the last words is consistent with the nature of the play. When he explains the meaning of the oracle's message, he is not only acting like one who works out a cryptic crossword clue, but he is also allowing us to recognize the mode of the action which we have witnessed. *Cymbeline* is primarily a play which taps conventional romance expectations, and the oracle is a signal that when expectations are fulfilled (however much they have been playfully exploited along the way), our admiration should be based on the thoroughly Aristotelian grounds that the dramatist has provided us with a surprise which is fully justified by the detail of the action. Self-consciously speaking for the dramatist and drawing attention to the skill of the plotter, Cymbeline reminds us of the careful verisimilitude which lies behind the revelations of the ending:

> O rare instinct!
> When shall I hear all through? This fierce abridgment
> Hath to it circumstantial branches, which
> Distinction should be rich in.
>
> (V.v.382–5)

And this exclamation is the prelude to a host of circumstantial questions and explanations which we are spared, for we know the answers already, and we can trust the characters to live in happiness forever afterwards.

I have argued it is important to recognize that the dominant mode of *Cymbeline* is romance, whatever other elements, more or less naturalistic, are included in its ample gaze. Some critics have reminded us that the historical and chronicle aspects are important,[17] while others have examined the qualities of irony, satire, and burlesque which introduce problems of audience response.[18] Although nobody has tried to argue the case, there might be something to say about the tragic potential in the play for it is placed at the end of the Tragedies in the Folio and contains a genuinely disturbing presentation of different versions of evil. The furthest that commentators who stress this side will go is to analyze the play as tragicomedy.[19] It should be clear from my total analysis in other chapters that although comedy may be basically an inherently exclusive category, romance is essentially a synthesizing genre, able to include in its structure a whole range of literary experiences which we normally try to isolate into other categories. There is nothing wrong, then, and much right, in saying that *Cymbeline* is predominantly a romance which nurses under its warm wings a variety of hatched eggs, including history, pastoral, tragedy, irony, and realism. We need not dismiss with ridicule Polonius's description of mixed modes for it points towards the very stuff of romance. *Cymbeline* may be difficult for modern audiences fully to grasp since we may be too determined to think dualistically, wanting to find a play comedy *or* tragedy, sentimental *or* satiric, romance *or* history, and so on. We cannot really know just how much delight a Jacobean, coterie theatre, priding itself on its chic sophistication in finding subtle literary jokes could also (like literary clichés everywhere?) allow itself a safe and full-blooded sentimentality, so long as the jokes and satire can be kept "in the family". We find such a narrow but real inclusiveness in other plays of the time and perhaps also in the 1890s and in Huxley's 1920s, amongst other periods. *Pericles* is the most universal and serious romance Shakespeare wrote. *Cymbeline* is the most Jacobean.

The Winter's Tale

At first sight Robert Greene's short romance, *Pandosto: The Triumph of Time*, offers no more to the dramatist than any other such work of the time and perhaps less than, for example, Lodge's *Rosalynde*. The latter is a much more compact story with some unity of place, time, and action, and considerable insight into the characters' minds. *Pandosto* pretends to be little more than its announcement claims:

> Pleasant for age to avoyde drowsie thoughtes, profitable for youth to eschue other wanton pastimes, and bringing to both a desired content.[20]

It does offer a little moral:

> Wherein is discovered by a pleasant Historie, that although by the meanes of sinister fortune, Truth may be concealed yet by Time in spight of fortune it is most manifestly revealed.

The narrative moves in episodic fashion through a series of events presented in linear order, and the overall direction is away from and back towards the oracle's statement, a device that takes much of the pressure from the writer to provide a more complex unity. The true deity behind the story is Fortune, the patron saint of romance:

> Fortune, who al this while has shewed a frendly face, began now to turne her back, and to shewe a lowring countenance . . .[21]

Greene brings back the living, the lost princess, but he cannot deliver the dead queen from her grave, so drastically would this threaten his carefully established verisimilitude. Time that takes away cannot always bring back. Eager to play according to the rules of literary theory, he emphasizes the element of poetic justice in an event that goes completely against the grain of the feelings, for after allowing his king complete happiness in a "comicall" ending, he perfunctorily kills Pandosto off as punishment for his earlier lustful thoughts towards his own daughter:

> . . . moved with these desperate thoughts, he fell into a melancholie fit, and to close up the Comedie with a Tragicall stratageme, he slewe himself.[22]

Out of such a modest, sprawling romance, Shakespeare creates a play which nowadays is regarded as a very great achievement, a work which hovers on the religious in its serious treatment of profoundly important themes.[23]

The pattern of *The Winter's Tale* is the familiar shape of romance, oscillating between joy and disaster, taking its inner sanction from the words of Time, disarmingly simple in their form and content yet bearing a wealth of Shakespearean thinking about the simultaneity of short time and long time built into the "endless ending":

> I, that please some, try all, both joy and terror
> Of good and bad, that makes and unfolds error,
> Now take upon me, in the name of Time,
> To use my wings. . . .
>
> . . .
> I witness to
> The times that brought them in; so shall I do
> To th'freshest things now reigning, and make stale
> The glistering of this present, as my tale
> Now seems to it.
>
> (IV.i.1–14 *passim*)

This is explicitly the voice of the dramatist himself "in the name of Time" speaking of his own tale, reminding us that its shape and set of significances are his own. In this play the new and important element is the concentration upon the existence of unlocated sin in the world of romance, which makes towards a teasingly relative presentation of morality, defying the existence of absolutes except in a prelapsarian world. Using the terms in a sense larger than the strictly Christian, the play proceeds by giving us first a glimpse of childhood paradise, whisking us then into a world of paradise lost where even innocence itself is dubious, then re-presenting and again destroying a different version of paradise in the pastoral world, and finally coming to rest on a Miltonic vision of paradise regained, a state of relative but solitary happiness, acknowledged to be fragile and a wonderful gift:

> They hand in hand with wandering steps and slow,
> Through Eden took their solitary way.

The last scene of the play, like that last picture of Adam and Eve, presents an ensemble of "precious winners all" (V.iii.131) who are held together in a willed fashion by their common acknowledgement of death (Paulina's husband), irretrievable loss of the innocent world, and an acceptance of personal responsibility which is constantly vigilant against the possibility of inadvertent error or sin. As in *Paradise Lost*, awareness of the fortune and misfortune that knowledge can bring lies at the heart of this play, the last in which Shakespeare fully enacts during the action the pattern of romance.

The glimpse of paradise at the beginning is as brief as a flower of spring, as intangible as a memory, and it forks almost instantly with a word. The childhood friendship between Leontes and Polixenes is said to have been so radiantly innocent that it "cannot choose but branch now". As Blake would remind us, the difference between innocence and experience can be discovered in how different minds may hear a single word: the innocent mind will see in "branch" a hopeful metaphor of the maturing tree while the mind that has left innocence will detect an ambiguity that points towards division. The scene that follows begins by leaving the ambiguity unresolved, but with the intrusion of Leontes' verbalized jealousy, we are plunged into a maelstrom of a morally ambiguous world. All critical discussions about the preparedness of Leontes' feelings are not quite to the point. The event is presented as a violent and abrupt explosion of the irrational (in all its menacing and obsessively rigorous logic) into a world which could have been relaxed and innocent. One could equally well examine the violent outburst of Polixenes in the pastoral scene and ask whether it is prepared for. The answer would be the same: such intrusions are, and remain, irrational. Immediately the early scene is clouded with the potential for two different perspectives on the same facts. Hermione *is* innocent, Leontes *is* guilty, and yet the powerful self-righteousness of his attack leads us at least to recognize the dangerousness and self-aware experience of the woman's amply relaxed sensuality of language:

> . . . cram's with praise, and make's
> As fat as tame things. One good deed dying tongueless
> Slaughters a thousand waiting upon that.
> Our praises are our wages; you may ride's
> With one soft kiss a thousand furlongs ere
> With spur we heat an acre.
>
> (I.ii.91–6)

By comparing this language with her dignified and lofty self-defense in the dock later, full of cleansed language, we realize that there are two meanings even in the word "innocence", the one opposed to guiltiness, the other opposed to experience. Similarly, Mamillius *is* innocent as a child, and yet we can find in his words about the ladies who paint their faces a precocious knowingness that taints the paradise which his childhood could represent. A part of our minds registers also that if there is a truly immature and blindly innocent person in the scene, it is Leontes himself, the one who, above all, embodies at this time the corrosive worm of experience which can color even the most harmless incidents with a darkening color of pollution. The whole scene upsets any easy moral categories we should choose to apply, just as effectively as do the writings of Blake and Nietzsche. It does, however, allow us at least to hang on to some touchstone of virtue, which acts as an anchor of decency. In this regard, the character of Camillo acts as a quiet monitor for our responses. Through him especially we comprehend that a terrible injustice is being perpetrated by Leontes, not wilfully but almost ignorantly. Looking back over the first half of *The Winter's Tale,* Time's phrase, "both joy and terror of good and bad" takes on the complexity of a syntax that could act as balanced parallels, balanced opposites, or a completely paradoxical chiasmus.

It is perhaps important to notice that in the first part of the play the literary reminiscence which lies closest to the surface is surprisingly not the jealousy of Othello but the tyranny of Lear. Whereas Othello appears to be mature and firmly secure in his love for Desdemona, requiring the constant provocations of Iago to unsettle his conviction, Leontes, like Lear, holds the seeds of his own disaster by relying simply upon the office of his own authority. Even when attempting to hold Polixenes in Sicilia, his words are closer to coercion than to the language of hospitality, and he also orders his Queen, "Speak you" (I.ii.27). Hermione's distinction between a guest and a prisoner is a shrewd way of distancing herself from her husband's tone, and Polixenes can respond more easily to her. She is "Not your gaoler then, But your kind hostess," words which may hold mild reproof for her husband's words of "invitation". When Leontes mutters "At my request he would not" (I.ii.87), he might more accurately have used the word "demand". The most striking aspect of the action up to the death of Mamillius is that nobody will obey Leontes' orders, for first one, then another and another disobey him. On seeing the play in performance it can appear that this, rather than any incipient jealousy, is what unsettles Leontes and goads him to a final frenzy when he attempts a last, most terrible assertion of his authority by ordering the gods about:

> There is no truth at all i' th' oracle.
> The sessions shall proceed. This is mere falsehood.
> (III.ii.137–8)

The words, "disobedience", "tyrannous", and "injustice" are on the lips of many people at this stage, and one cannot help feeling that the issue is not so much bound up with sex and psychology as more fundamentally with a political question where a king is demanding obedience for its own sake to legitimize his precarious authority. More generally the feeling is that Leontes is attempting to coerce more wide and non-human forces such as truth and time into a petty form of obedience. The rest of the play shows that not even a king can do this.[24]

As if to wash away in the most definitive and forceful way possible the murkiness and moral relativity of the claustrophobic court, the dramatist simply disposes of all his characters, retrieving only the most innocent, the newborn babe, in order to start all over again from the beginning in the hope that it will be different this time. Critics who find a subtle interrelatedness between the two "parts" of this play are, of course, partially correct, for it would not add up to one play but two if there were not parallels and connections. But it seems equally necessary to stress the obvious unconnectedness in order to find what the play is doing. Shakespeare is allowing his characters the possibility of avoiding retribution from the past by denying its existence. He gives his dramatic world a second chance. Two characters — Mamillius and Antigonus — are defiantly killed off as sacrifices to the affronted gods; Hermione is killed off to Leontes to enable him to find agonizingly slow repentance through grief, without having to live with the palpable facts of his blindness in the daily existence of a wife whose identity he has betrayed conclusively; and Leontes is killed off to us, consigned to a tomb of self-immolation and stagnancy. Nothing could be so decisive. Nothing could be so beautifully hopeful as the fresh start, garlanded with the strawberries of unworried, rustic celebration, quickened with the vitality and exquisitely liquid poetry of young love. Long time, the time that governs with leisure the change of seasons, the time that enables the very old shepherd recalling his dead wife to mingle with the very young dreaming of their unborn children, is slipped in to allow us to forget the explosive violence of a time that was too short for reflection, recollection or forethought. Regarded in this light, *The Winter's Tale* becomes an almost schematic presentation of the notion of the "endless ending". First there is the example of short time, consummated as it must be with death. Then the vista of long time, transcending mortality with larger rhythms, is gently evoked as in the earlier comedies in the celebration of a day that contains agelessness. In the third movement of the sonata form the two modes are interfaced in a way that evokes nostalgia and hope, joy and melancholy, the past and the future.

The splicing of the two dimensions comes during the long, pastoral scene like a gradual but then sudden awakening. It comes as a perception that mortals cannot live as if they are fully accommodated within the immortal rhythms. Only gods and art can withstand, as effectively as Keats's Grecian urn, the tug of the past and the necessity of an individual life ending in death. Perdita herself throughout the scene expresses the sense of living on borrowed time. "Goddess-like pranked up" she knows her situation is a disguise, and she can barely believe in the wonder of impersonating the immortals. She is unsurprised, though naturally disappointed, when Polixenes, an obvious relic of the old world of the court, full of spitefulness and the destructiveness of people living too close to their own mortality, destroys the second chance given to the dramatic world:

> This dream of mine —
> Being now awake, I'll queen it no inch further,
> But milk my ewes, and weep.
>
> (IV.iv.440-2)

But just as the ending of the first section was too decisive to be true, so is her despair too pessimistic, and once again the trusty rudder to guide the characters towards a muted but hopeful reconciliation is good old Camillo. He works very hard as the dramatist-within-the-machine for he acts not only as plotter when the story gets tangled but also as a firm guide for our moral sympathies. He will never let go his wise and practical understanding of each character, and like time itself he will never unequivocally abandon anything.

As in the other plays in which we are given an ageing figure at the center, the dominant feeling at every point in the romance section is that something is gained as something is lost. Leontes seems to feel at first that what is lost as one grows is some quality of innocence embodied in the child. His notion is somewhat Wordsworthian, that as we grow away from childhood we grow away from the center, relinquishing the splendor in the grass for a more threatening knowledge of the world which in his case is specifically sexual. Hermione and Paulina, however, through the situation in which they are placed, can be forgiven for believing that what is lost is not some mystical quality but particular items of human love and value: a child, a reputation, love itself, a husband, and sixteen years of living time. Leontes must learn a hard but necessary lesson by losing sixteen years also, as well as a wife for a time and a child forever. Perdita, however, represents all that is gained at the same time for she is maturing as the others are in a state of immobility, and she is linked to the dark times when she was gestating in the womb and the time darker still when she was born in an unlucky hour. The curious but beautiful little interchange between the lovers when Florizel and Perdita joke about flowers strewn upon a corpse is romantic and natural in its context, but it holds also a subtle symbolism which springs directly from the imaginative or visionary center of the play. Even the old Shepherd in his evocation of "the Breughelesque heartiness of the peasant wife"[25] indicates in his words the rhythm of losing and gaining (a wife and a daughter respectively, a time of rough bonhomie and a tone of more courtly refinement), which is so central to the development of the play as a whole. From this point of view, another image holds a delicately pregnant symbolic quality:

> When you do dance, I wish you
> A wave o' th' sea, that you might ever do
> Nothing but that; move still, still so,
> And own no other function.
>
> (IV.i.v.140–3)

The waves of time may gather and break, but their presence is eternal in the unchanging stillness of the water itself, rocking up and down.

Just as the last Act is the final movement of three in the play, so it contains in itself three distinct sections, all dwelling in different ways upon the connection between the past and the present in recognition of the absolute loss of innocence. Each part focuses on a different character as its center, first

Leontes, then Perdita, and finally Hermione. Leontes is found immobilized, just as was Pericles, but in this case it is not loss but conscience which is paralyzing him. He is now suffering from his own past actions and the guilt they engendered, like an Othello who happened to live on. Paulina acts as a sometimes vindictive mouthpiece for the nemesis within Leontes himself. She relentlessly taunts him with his knowledge of guilt, harping upon "she you killed" (v.i.15) and never allowing him for a moment to escape the mesh of his personal suffering. Stridently, shrilly, she accuses both Leontes and Cleomenes of degrading the memory of the dead queen while they are admiring the beauty of Perdita. When she insists upon hammering home a reminder that the young Florizel is the same age as his own son would have been, Leontes all but snaps under the intolerably oppressive pressure:

> Prithee no more; cease. Thou know'st
> He dies to me again when talk'd of.
>
> (v.i.118–9)

Judged as a dramatic character, Paulina cannot be seen as cruel since she reveals herself as the final agent of providence in restoring Leontes' wife, and she has ample cause for personal resentment and grief at her own loss of a husband who cannot be resurrected. The potential cruelty in her words and in her complete preoccupation with the dead queen stems from the suffering in Leontes' own mind, caused by his acceptance of personal responsibility and guilt. The court at this stage is full of the feeling of shame immediately after the Fall. Paradise is well and truly lost, without redemption, and knowledge is no more than unadulterated suffering. The imposition of the short time of the individual consciousness leads to the notion that there is nothing left except death since the one means of atonement, the possibility of a new innocent relationship with his own wife or with anybody else, is explicitly denied by Paulina's gnomic comments.

Like a cliché, the entrance into this world of Florizel, Perdita, and their unlikely entourage of shepherds and a rogue heralds the intervention of the potential for a future. They call up the hopefulness of youth, the seasonal cycles of the shepherd's life, and the personal renewal involved in self-forgetfulness:

> Welcome hither,
> As is the spring to th'earth!
>   (v.i.151–2)

> The blessed gods
> Purge all infection from our air whilst you
> Do climate here!
>   (v.i.168–70)

The reconciliation between Leontes and his daughter is reported to us by the rather dandyish, stylish Gentlemen of the court. Many commentators have pointed out that this device allows Shakespeare to move quickly on to his great dénouement without giving it the sense of an anticlimax,[26] but there may be other reasons for the choice of presentation. This particular reunion is very close to a romantic cliché in itself, repeating the formula of *Pericles* except that in the former case greater significance could be attached to Marina's own personal acquisition of a past, parallel to her father's retrieval of a past. In *The Winter's Tale* the restoration of Perdita is irrelevant to the guilty suffering of Leontes, and in fact it can do little more than intensify his own knowledge of a crime against his lost wife. Pericles had been guiltless, and so his daughter is a divine gift which allows him to live again, connected again with his past. Leontes is presented as overwhelmingly guilty, and his daughter is a continuing sign of his past guilt and a further enforcement of grief since it does not affect the kind of suffering which he has been undergoing. For this reason, the reconciliation between father and daughter is presented in a mode very close to parody, for the language of the Gentlemen is self-regarding and euphuistically old-fashioned. Shakespeare is not simply "saving up" his climax. He is recognizing that this incident, although essential for the completion of the plot, is potentially emotionally distracting, and he is carefully skirting the problem.

With astonishing economy[27] the final scene of *The Winter's Tale* effects the most intricate and comprehensive presentation of the wedding between long time and short in any of the

Shakespearean romance plays. The scene leads us, as Michael leads Adam, into a state of mystical awareness of the limitations and infinity of time itself:

> He ended; and thus Adam last replied.
> How soon hath thy prediction, seer blast,
> Measured this transient world, the race of time,
> Till time stand fixed: beyond is all abyss,
> Eternity, whose end no eye can reach.[28]

Shakespeare reaches this "top of speculation" by giving to each character a distinct significance in the patterns of time. The passage of time represented in the play is, first, the lifespan of one man, Leontes, up to one moment in old age. The gathering references to death point us towards the discreteness of an individual life, from birth to death. Hermione, too, ages even while absent from the living world. Within this passage, however, there is another pattern of individual time, for Leontes has quite clearly not been "living" since the death of his wife. He has been immobilized in remorse and memory. Therefore, the bulk of the play represents a vacuum in living, beginning with the end of vitality and ending with its resumption in the personal history of Leontes. Perhaps this is one of the organic reasons for the disappearance of Leontes and Hermione during the middle of the action. Beyond the lifespan we have the family-span. The first scene of the play resurrects a time when Leontes was a child in his own family; then it reminds us of a time before he was married; then we see the growth to maturity of his own progeny; and the ending of the play shows us the family altogether for the first time — a point of passing time which is also a mid-point in an eternal pattern, for the family is a continuity that absorbs and rides above the lives of its individual members. Finally, within and above the spans of the personal life and the span of the family lies the pattern from life to death and death to life, linked with the cycles of nature. Hermione, Perdita, and Leontes have all been metaphorically "dead" for a space and by the end they are living once again. The scene begins by stirring memories, and proceeds in a way that, having "conjured to remembrance" (V.iii.40) memories from the past, now miraculously conjures the dead past into a living vein. Hermione, in par-

ticular, is most spectacularly "stol'n from the dead". Many of
these reverberating, overlapping patterns of time are mysteriously evoked in the strangest lines of all, as Paulina practices
her lawful art in allowing so many people to resume their
living existences:

> 'Tis time; descend; be stone no more; approach;
> Strike all that look upon with marvel. Come;
> I'll fill your grave up. Stir; nay, come away.
> Bequeath to death your numbness, for from him
> Dear life redeems you.
>
> (V.iii.98–103)

Memory of death belongs to the past, not the future, but there
is for each individual another death in the future which is
final. This string had been touched lightly at many points —
Autolycus's jaunty observation, "For the red blood reigns in
the winter's pale" (IV.iii.4) and in the lust for life of the young
Perdita wanting to garland her lover with flowers:

FLORIZEL: What, like a corse?
PERDITA: No; like a bank for love to lie and play on;
        Not like a corse; or if – not to be buried,
        But quick, and in mine arms.

> (IV.iv.129–32)

In the final scene there is no simplicity or generalization about
the merging attitudes to time, since they are lived through on
the pulses of people caught up in time, including us as the
witnesses to these miracles of art. Such a mode of living art
prevents us from extracting any abstract statement of theme,
for we too are ones in this interlude. With Pygmalion in mind,
Shakespeare achieves a resurrection that art can bring on
various levels. He stands as Julio Romano to the story of
Pandosto by Greene, retrieving it from its grave of obscurity in
the 1580s, quickening it into life by placing its fable in a
medium that demands performance by living people.
Furthermore, by changing its ending with the revival of
Hermione, he is bringing life in a literal sense to a story which
in its source had closed with death, so that every performance
will conclude on a note of hard-won hope, freeing its characters to go on into an existence of renewed relationships and

shared vitality. Once again, the Grecian urn is not far behind, as the play teases us out of thought as doth eternity, its marble lady living and yet not living, the play ending and yet not ending.

Paulina and Camillo are married off. Is this yet another perfunctory convenience to round off the plot, leaving no threads loose? To some extent it is, but even such an interpretation holds a special appropriateness for these two characters. Camillo has guided one part of the plot with adroitness throughout. He has gently allowed the play to hold onto the living at dangerous moments, awaiting the time when they can all be brought together. Like a skilful navigator he has sustained the plot at its riskiest moments. Meanwhile, Paulina has been equally expert in holding onto the other side of the plot, the preservation of Hermione and the humbling of Leontes, and she has superbly stage-managed the reconciliation at the end. When these two characters are paired off, we are invited to consider how similar their roles throughout have been, and we can see the liaison as having been somehow implicit throughout. They can now be afforded a congratulatory handshake and a mutual reward from the grandmaster of the plot, the dramatist himself.

With such considerations, the plot has become an artifice which we can stand back and contemplate in all its wonderful craft and artistry. And yet, such consideration does not lead to a knowledge of the artist himself nor even a recognition of his existence behind the work. The play as it is experienced through time is the creation of nobody in particular, and it comes alive not only by what it gives us but also by what we give to it. Paulina carefully prepares her spectators for a co-operative enterprise which involves both the work of art and the feelings of the perceivers, as she brings a "statue" to life. Her comments are explicit enough as advice to readers and theatre audiences as well as to her stage audience:

> It is requir'd
> You do awake your faith. Then all stand still;
> Or those that think it is unlawful business
> I am about, let them depart.

(V.iii.94–7)

From an artist who once boasted that his way is to conjure us, this comes as a humble confession that the work will not live, and his conjuring will be unlawful, if we will not help in its re-creation every time we read or see the play. Such a comment is perhaps true of all art but it has most pertinence to the mode of romance, which is in some ways so artificial and purely imaginary that it may be hooted at like an old tale, or judged simply from the outside as a static artefact. We recall Bottom's garbled allusion to the biblical quotation advising us to allow the rational parts of our mind to sleep, and awaken our faith in the existence and truth of mysteries. With the mutual involvement of the perceivers which Paulina pleads for, the romance will be a fulfilment of our own best emotional desires, our most generous wish for the future happiness of the greatest number of people. *The Winter's Tale* follows the hard-won victories of *All's Well That Ends Well* and *Antony and Cleopatra* by enacting an order of providence that may become our own: by seeing the best, by wishing for the best, we may create the best.

No doubt, as philosophers, physicists, and literary critics often remind us, there are many ways in which time can be described and apprehended. In some abstract sense, they may all be simultaneously true. However, for an individual on a particular occasion, only one may be supremely understood. On a sharp, clear morning in spring, it might seem that time is essentially cyclical, for we have come back to the moment we have been waiting for, its fresh optimism remembered from a twelvemonth before. On a long summer's afternoon, the primary feeling may be that time is endless, and thoughts of an ending are as faint as the moon on the blue sky. At twilight on a winter's day, finality and the specter of death may be immediate and real. One's own position on the spectrum between youth and age will have a bearing, for hope and memory are powerful faculties. In Shakespearean romances, we find many of these dimensions present and equally true, for they are fully felt by individuals. Florizel and Perdita may trust to long time while Leontes, having experienced the horrors of wasting time so that time wastes him, has been given a precious reprieve; Pericles finds his long memory brought back in reality in the persons of a wife and daughter. It is, in short, the triumph of the mode of romance that it brings events to fulfilment without enforcing the sense that time stops for everybody on the occasion of an important event for one or two people — marriage in comedy, death in tragedy. We may relax into its kindly, ample atmosphere, secure in the knowledge that such a way of perceiving reality is no facile illusion but is true to the world as it is.[30]

VII The Tempest

On the surface, *The Tempest* is a montage of romance materials. There is a magician, a fairy, spirits of the air who create beautiful music, a monster, two young people who fall in love, a villain, and a storm. At the same time, however, the play seems to inhabit a world very different from that of the three romances which we have just examined, and it demands a different treatment. Obeying the classical unities strictly, there is only one setting, a remote and alien island, and we do not have within the action of the play the expanses of time through seasonal cycles or from the birth to death of a character which we find in the romance world. There are reminiscences and premonitions, but these point to times taken up before and after the sequence of events in the play. There is an aloof classicism which pulls against the romance elements, imposing a sense of stasis upon a medium which, as we have seen, deals centrally with change and flux. The classical control and allusiveness are at their most prominent in the scene which is the most magical of all, the marriage masque created by Prospero's spirits. All this adds up to the feeling that *The Tempest* is a very strange play, full of diverse elements brought into unity, and nowhere is its strangeness manifested so powerfully as in its "sense of an ending". Most critics who have written on *The Tempest* confess themselves eventually, like Henry James, "baffled and exasperated" by the play's opacity. We are not guided by a reliable and central consciousness, and we do not seem to be in touch with the artist behind the work:

> . . . the artist is so steeped in the abysmal objectivity of his characters and situations that the great billows of the medium itself play with him, to our vision, very much as, over a ship's side, in certain waters, we catch, through transparent waters, the flash of strange sea-creatures.[1]

To take a plunge, however, in order to find a point of entrance into the play, we might concentrate upon the various levels of ambiguity and relativity which have already been hinted at.

First, *The Tempest* is ambiguous in its *genre*, even more so than the "problem" comedies. It is not a full-fledged romance, since conflict and the vicissitudes of fortune lie in the past rather than in the action. The play has a "happy ending" but it leaves us with forgiveness which is begrudging,[2] and a protagonist whose every third thought will be the grave. To see it as a pastoral romance based on Longus's *Daphnis and Chloe* may reveal several specific parallels[3] as well as reminding us of the pastoral arc under which characters enter the magic place of contemplation and eventually leave for the world of action. But again, such awareness is of limited value. Equally, the play yields few of its secrets to the scholar of sources since, lacking one central identifiable source, it fleetingly adverts to a great diversity of works, both fictional and factual.[4] A thorough examination might reveal that many significant sources are the words of Shakespeare himself, glimpsed from earlier plays in the dark backward and abysm of time. At every corner, we detect some echo of a familiar Shakespearean cadence or thought.[5] But simply to see the play as a consummation, as a self-reflective exercise designed to complete and close the record of Shakespeare's development, falsifies the utter sense of novelty, originality and new directions. Our first concession to the play's difficulty must be to say that, while including aspects of every genre, it belongs to none in particular. "The great billows of the medium itself," poetic drama, ride over more narrow classifications.

Like Beckett's *Endgame*, *The Tempest* can be said partly to be "about" the medium of art itself as it moves through time, and centrally about an ending. Virtually from the opening moments we feel ourselves to be in the presence of an ending in the comic-romance world. The storm is equivalent to the crisis which precipitates the relevations in the last Acts in such plays as *The Two Gentlemen of Verona* (the violence in the forest), *Much Ado About Nothing* (the incipient violence in Beatrice's 'Kill Claudio!'), *Twelfth Night* (the fights that break out as Act V opens), and *Measure for Measure* (the angry public denunciations that greet the Duke's return). The ensemble is gathered together to be separated only temporarily. The controlling Duke-figure has events in his grip even more firmly than in other plays because he is quickly shown to be a magician even more powerful than the one acknowledged by Rosalind as she begins to manipulate the ending. Prospero is as brooding, time-bound, and self-reflective as Leontes or the King in *All's Well that Ends Well*, and like them he is stirring the waters of memory as he speaks to Miranda of the past. The spirit of wonder characteristic of the romance ending is stirred in the first Act by Ariel's serene songs, so "rich and strange" in themselves, and Ferdinand is as rapt by the dream-like quality of the isle as the lovers are spellbound at the end of *A Midsummer Night's Dream*: "My spirits, as in a dream, are all bound up" (I.ii.486). This sense of wonder never slackens, as if the final movement of *As You Like It* has been extended to cover a whole play. Finally, we are in no doubt from the time of Prospero's fevered re-telling of his tale to Miranda with a tone as guilt-stricken and compulsive as the Ancient Mariner's, that there are good people and bad people who have been assembled for the purpose of achieving poetic justice. The issues that usually take four Acts to clarify and come to a head are, in *The Tempest*, swiftly unveiled in the opening moments. At the same time, however, we detect various countermovements. Although the characters are engaged in a sustained ending, they equally have not yet begun living for until Prospero sorts out the problems, he cannot resume his dukedom in Milan. Ariel, although buoyant, is trapped, and looks forward to a freedom which will begin his true existence as an independent spirit. Caliban is continually attempting to escape and begin a new life. Moreover, beyond even the patterns that make the play an ending and a beginning, there is a powerful sense of the characters being imprisoned in the present. Whether Prospero looks back to the dark past or forward ultimately to his own death there seems no escape from an existence which is always "now" in the word repeated three times in the Epilogue.

The nature of *The Tempest* can be described only in a series of paradoxes: improbable yet naturalistic, static yet in perpetual motion, an ending which is a beginning, time-bound (observing the unities strictly), yet floating free in the timeless realm of symbolism, morally simple — a matter of blacks and whites — and yet equivocal and inconclusive, depicting grey areas of ethical choices which mingle forgiveness with resentment. In all its elegant simplicity the play shifts and turns like the ocean. Even the rhythms of the verse take up an ebb and flow, the surge of the long paragraph sucked back by the tug of the half-line.[6]

> There they hoist us,
> To cry to th' sea that roar'd to us; to sigh
> To th' winds, whose pity, sighing back again,
> Did us but loving wrong.
>
> (I.ii.148–51)
>
> Their understanding
> Begins to swell, and the approaching tide
> Will shortly fill the reasonable shore
> That now lies foul and muddy.
>
> (V.i.80–2)

Many writers have noticed that long contemplation of the sea may enable us to detach ourselves from human dealings in a way that makes them less significant than they seem. Keats, another great poet of the sea, captures as well as Shakespeare on the one hand its awesome remoteness and disinterest:

> It keeps eternal whisperings around
> Desolate shores, and with its mighty swell
> Gluts twice ten thousand caverns, till the spell
> Of Hecate leaves them their old shadowy sound.[7]

and on the other hand the sea's protective solicitude for the human world:

> The moving waters at their priestlike task
> Of pure ablution round earth's human shores.

The Tempest, washed by the music of the sea, sustains these two points of view: intense moments encountered on the "human shores" where people are caught up in their own social, moral, and emotional involvements, and simultaneously the "eternal whisperings" of a vast, amoral freedom which tends to trivialize human experiences. The play seems to hover between attentiveness to human distress and joy, and lofty neglect of true warmth. Some of the secrets are yielded up once we recognize the central image, the sea, in its state of unchanging change.

The double perspective extends to the moral and emotional world of the play where individual change is set against eternal patterns. Consider the presentation of the love affair between Miranda and Ferdinand. Shakespeare could easily have shown us the emotions and the romance of young love as he did in his earlier comedies, applying his eye to the telescope and dwelling upon the warmth and exclamatory wonder of a "brave new world" discovered by an individual under the promptings of quickening feelings. But instead, he places at our shoulder one who reverses the telescope and invokes the distance of recurrent human experience: "'Tis new to thee". There is the philosopher's reductiveness in Prospero's "At first sight they have changed eyes". Shakespeare could have magnanimously amplified the rich glow of new life in the young woman, but instead he chooses to trace the inception of experience seen as the discovery of something calculating and strategical, an exercise of power as old as human nature:

FERDINAND: Wherefore weep you?
MIRANDA: At mine unworthiness, that dare not offer
  What I desire to give, and much less take
  What I shall die to want. But this is trifling;
  And all the more it seeks to hide itself,
  The bigger bulk it shows. Hence, bashful cunning!
          (III.i.76–81)

In the innocence of her childhood Miranda is recalled as being a cherubin "that did preserve" Prospero with a smile "Infused with a fortitude from heaven." Now that she has reached the moment of budding experience, she is on the point of losing the capacity to represent heavenly hope to her father, and Prospero must surrender her in as positive a way as he must come to give Ariel freedom. For Prospero a relationship is ending, while for Miranda one is beginning. Paradoxically, each event manipulated into being by Prospero has the effect of isolating him from true contact with others, and it is a measure of the kindness and sadness of his actions that he knows this. At each stage of the play, for each character, something is gained, but at the expense of something lost. Meanwhile, in presenting Ferdinand Shakespeare could have made him into the eager, callow young man, absolute and exaggerated in his romantic affections of the early comedies. And yet he chooses to toss in the note of a profligate roué, who has tried the field in a coolly critical spirit and has decided it is time to "settle down":

> Full many a lady
> I have ey'd with best regard; and many a time
> Th'harmony of their tongues hath into bondage
> Brought my too diligent ear; for several virtues
> Have I lik'd several women; never any
> With so full soul, but some defect in her
> Did quarrel with the noblest grace she ow'd
> And put it to the foil.

> (III.i.39–46)

Shakespeare could have spiritualized the love itself or at least, as in *As You Like It*, included sexuality as its healthily fruitful adjunct. But instead he chooses to question sexual desire as a potentially destructive impulse. Prospero, perhaps suspecting Ferdinand as deeply as Polonius suspected Hamlet, shakes a warning finger:

> If thou dost break her virgin-knot before
> All sanctimonious ceremonies may
> With full and holy rite be minist'red,
> No sweet aspersion shall the heavens let fall
> To make this contract grow; but barren hate,
> Sour-ey'd disdain, and discord, shall bestrew
> The union of your bed with weeds so loathly
> That you shall hate it both.

> (IV.i.15–22)

As if this is not strong enough, the warning is repeated:

> Do not give dalliance
> Too much the rein; the strongest oaths are straw
> To th'fire i'th' blood. Be more abstemious,
> Or else, good night your vow!

> (IV.i.51–4)

The fear exists only in Prospero's vision, but something of its vehemence rubs off on our attitude to Ferdinand, as if there is an unspoken equation between him and Caliban whose great desire was to people the island by raping Miranda. The wave of association spreads further to taint even Miranda herself, for by implication it is her own involuntary and un-acknowledged beauty that inspires the chaos of lust. In Prospero's attitude we are reminded of Yeats's prayer for his daughter:

> May she be granted beauty, and yet not
> Beauty to make a stranger's eye distraught,
> Or hers before a looking-glass . . .

And again, more directly:

> And may her bridegroom bring her to a house
> Where all's accustomed, ceremonious;
> . . .
> How but in custom and in ceremony
> Are innocence and beauty born?[8]

Prospero can provide the "sanctimonious ceremonies", a decorous and distant work of art that celebrates marriage as a recurrent pattern in human society, governed by such ancient deities as Juno and Ceres. But the dangerous and volatile sense of newness of experience felt by young lovers in their emotions eludes the control of custom and ceremony. In the various emotions it stirs in different people, the marriage comes to be a ceremony that marks an ending and a beginning.

Hatred is as problematical and relative as love in the double perspective of *The Tempest*. Caliban hates Prospero as a capricious and vindictive tyrant. Prospero loathes and occasionally fears Caliban as an uncouth, rebellious, and un-grateful savage. And yet the two are connected in a curiously tight bond. Having taught Caliban how to speak, Prospero has taught him how to curse, and has created him partly in his own image to such an extent that he must admit "This thing of darkness I acknowledge mine." Caliban is the image of those areas in Prospero that he is too civilized and sociable to reveal. The threats posed to orderly existence — feelings of sexual desire, resentment, a bitter need for revenge and for power — all lie within the magician himself, so disquietingly recalcitrant that they can be kept at bay only by willed domination and self-control, occasionally popping out in moments of irrational anger or "trouble". On the occasions when the muddy waters of memory are stirred, when "the dark backward and abysm of time" brings to the surface things which have lain dormant below the threshold of consciousness, Prospero finds himself close to Caliban, driven by feelings rather than by patterns of reason, angrily resentful over the way his brother usurped power so many years before. On the other hand, no matter how deficient in decorous civility or willed repression Caliban may be, no matter how full of curses and anger, he has positive attributes which Prospero lacks. He has feelings of true generosity, a tenderness eager to reach out to those who have not yet betrayed him, and he has an eloquent oneness with the nature of the island. He knows "every *fertile* inch o'the island", while Prospero seems weary of its barrenness. Caliban knows its fertility and living qualities with delighted intimacy:

> I'll show thee the best springs; I'll pluck thee berries;
> I'll fish for thee, and get thee wood enough.
>
>   . . .
>
> I prithee let me bring thee where crabs grow;
> And I with my long nails will dig thee pignuts;
> Show thee a jay's nest, and instruct thee how
> To snare the nimble marmoset; I'll bring thee
> To clust'ring filberts, and sometimes I'll get thee
> Young scamels from the rock.
>
> (II.ii.149–62 *passim*)

The courteousness of his address, couched in its deferential "thee", is sincere rather than a forced or acquired mannerism. His eager precision of detail, his identification with the natural world remind us that not only was the island Caliban's before Prospero arrived but also that in a sense it still is. The warmth of feeling behind his offer makes the language of Prospero's masque with its "rich leas" and "turfy mountains where live nibbling sheep" distantly classical, tame, and literary, as if anticipating the pastoral patterning of

"L'Allegro" and "Il Penseroso" but not even scratching the surface of a place in which he has lived for thirteen years. Prospero remembers his books but has not observed with his eyes nor awakened his warmer feelings. However beautiful in its classical restraint and delicate rhythms, Prospero's masque is as inappropriate to its setting, as coolly unfeeling, as a performance of Noel Coward for a white audience in the middle of Africa.

Hatred and contempt also exist between Prospero and the man who is the real "villain" of the piece, Antonio. Here again, there is some kind of deep association between the two, based to some extent on shared qualities, and to some extent on mutual envy. Both are inclined to treat people as commodities, for just as Antonio remains superciliously aloof from Alonso and Gonzalo, plotting to take their lives and power, so does Prospero plot to seize power, and so does he bully Ferdinand and his own agents, Caliban and Ariel. He is reproved by Ariel for a lapse in human sympathy, and since the reprimand comes from a spirit with no feelings at all, it is a sharper indictment even than Miranda's tearful pleas to her father to mollify the suffering of the shipwrecked newcomers and later of her lover. The real threat from Antonio, however, lies in a capacity which Prospero does not fully have — consistent emotional self-containment and *truly* cold imperviousness to feelings even of anger and resentment. It is this makes Antonio immune to Prospero's magic. He cannot hear the beautiful music, he sees the ground not as fertile but as tawny, and he cannot be put to sleep as the others can. His very charmlessness is an uncharmability that presents as potent a magic in its own right as Prospero's, showing up an element of impotent tricksiness in the latter. W. H. Auden, in his re-creation of *The Tempest*, *The Sea and the Mirror*, shows Antonio contemptuously laughing at Prospero, seeing *him* as the "poor worm", infected by petty pride:

> Your all is partial, Prospero;
>   My will is all my own:
> Your need to love shall never know
> Me: I am I, Antonio,
>   By choice alone.[9]

Antonio stands as an image for the black tyrant Prospero *could* be if he had less "need to love" and also for the consistently undisturbed man Prospero cannot be, and in both cases there is a sinister link between the two.

Prospero's moral status, then, is of a highly ambiguous kind, fitting the nature of the play. Never fully allowing us into his confidence, retiring when he is "troubled" instead of giving a voice to his anxieties, there is an Iago-like opaqueness about his motives which means that we must take his benevolence somewhat on trust. He mirrors the faults and virtues of those around him while retaining the detachment of his own knowledge and experience which he cannot share with others. Throughout, his most individual aspect lies in a burdening awareness of his own unique memories and of his own approaching death. His presence casts across the play a wash of tired nostalgia, and a melancholy recognition of the poignant transience of life, as of art:

> These our actors,
> As I foretold you, were all spirits, and
> Are melted into air, into thin air;
> And, like the baseless fabric of this vision,
> The cloud-capp'd towers, the gorgeous palaces,
> The solemn temples, the great globe itself,
> Yea, all which it inherit, shall dissolve,
> And like this insubstantial pageant faded,
> Leave not a rack behind. We are such stuff
> As dreams are made on; and our little life
> Is rounded with a sleep.
>
> (IV.i.148–58)

Prospero is, as moment follows moment, increasingly limited by his own irreversible and thickening experience which increasingly denies him the possibility of *surprise*. He can "foretell" everything, having observed it all before, to such an extent that he is in a godlike position of control, for he knows even those areas which he cannot control such as changeable emotions and death. The knowledge that experience brings strangely limits the area of spontaneous action; it necessitates the giving up of many things one by one; it is a state of decreasing potential; and it is the gradual inception of an

awareness that things are about to end for his own consciousness. It is significant that many of the characters sleep
at some stage during the play, and more significant that
afterwards they would prefer not to have woken up. A state of
true innocence, of living without an awareness of passing time,
can be only half-remembered, as a dream, if it actually ever
existed, for experience is a state defined by the very fact that in
our acquired knowledge of recurrent patterns we have a sense
of the past and the future. Caliban, subhuman yet centrally
human, speaks for them all:

> . . . and then, in dreaming,
> The clouds methought would open and show riches
> Ready to drop upon me, that, when I wak'd
> I cried to dream again.
>
> (III.ii.135–8)

While Prospero looks back upon the patterns of experience
which he can now read like a book with the hindsight of "long
time", most of the other characters are involved in en-
countering the world for the first time. They are involved in
living the dream world of "now", but they cannot yet see it *as*
a dream. For them, the action may be a beginning. For
Prospero, it is an ending.

There is one character who escapes both the sense of life's
novelty and the crushing weight of cumulative experience and
the burden of an impending ending. Like a bubble, Ariel rises
to the surface of the ocean, and disappears into thin air.
Because he is a spirit, he has no feelings, no alternative states
of dreaming and wakefulness, no development from innocence
to experience, no independent capacity for good or evil. His
history reveals not a movement away from freedom along the
clogging path of knowledge and experience towards the death
which Prospero anticipates, but instead an expansion outwards, towards limitless space. He was freed from the oak tree
in which he had been trapped by the wicked witch Sycorax, to
find himself less subservient but none the less in bondage, this
time to a white magician. He looks forward to true freedom, at
the beck and call of nobody, when the play has ended.
Whereas, for other characters, the play demonstrates a
movement towards a more limited role, a final assertion of

power before shedding it, and a reductive, generalizing tendency, Ariel's passage suggests a countermovement, and his presence shows the double perspective of the play in a different light. If Ariel is to "represent" anything, it seems to be something as undefined as creativity independent of the burden of human feelings or a sense of history. Although forced into the service of Prospero, required to act out his whims, the essential nature of Ariel is as separate from his master as a finished work of art is separate from its creator. A writer can create only from his own experience, and this will inevitably be limited by his own time and fashion of existence.But as he creates, some impulse — call it imagination — is reaching to transcend the merely personal (exacting a revenge, attracting a lover), yearning to chart a territory shared by all humanity at all times. While the artist reaches towards an ending, inspiration opens out into endlessness. If the Ariel in an artist does its job properly, then after the work is finished and the transient feelings have been represented, the object acquires a status that is independent of the feelings or occasion which prompted it, extending the experience into a timeless future. It becomes like the sea or the sun (or again, the Grecian Urn), disinterested and self-sufficient, and yet large enough to allow any perceiver to find his own personal and intimate relationship with it.

The songs of Ariel are cryptic statements about the process of creativity, and about the status of the serene self-assurance of the finished work of art which evades the narrow conclusiveness of an ending. At first he beckons us with an inveigling finger onto the magic island of art which is as controlled, as communal, and as delightful as the dance:

> Come unto these yellow sands,
>   And then take hands;
> Curtsied when you have and kiss'd
>   The wild waves whist,
> Foot it featly here and there,
> And, sweet sprites, the burden bear.
>   (I.i.375–80)

The poetry is drawing attention to the daintiness of its own metrical "feet", its own poetic "burden" carried by the sprites who are its characters, while inviting us to participate in its rhythms and dance in time with them. Next, Ariel reminds us of the crucial limitation of finished art. However aesthetically fascinating, it is essentially static and dead, a transmutation of one person's feelings and fluctuating experience into a jewellike object, free for all to contemplate but never stirred from its own dream:[10]

> Full fathom five thy father lies;
>   Of his bones are coral made;
> Those are pearls that were his eyes;
>   Nothing of him that doth fade
> But doth suffer a sea-change
> Into something rich and strange.
>
> (I.ii.396–401)

For each listener, the significance of these words will be different. Ferdinand is reminded of his father whom he thinks drowned. For us, who know that Alonso is alive, the song points to something larger concerning the nature of art. People like Antony and Cleopatra — or Shakespeare — may have once been living and breathing. Now they are dead, but what remains is a static representation of their moving experiences. They exist in an untouchable realm, pearly in their clarity and stillness. Ariel's third song looks forward to the most numinous realm of all, an even greater, mystical freedom. He sings in celebration of the *potential* for art that lies simply in the existence of the physical world as it breathes and moves even before an artist has found it or a person has noticed it:

> Where the bee sucks, there suck I;
> In a cowslip's bell I lie;
> There I couch when owls do cry.
> On the bat's back I do fly
> After summer merrily.
> Merrily, merrily, shall I live now,
> Under the blossom that hangs on the bough.
>
> (V.i.88–94)

Beauty — art without its static representation — is secret, delicate, and as endless as an eternal "now". As Emily Dickinson has said in a complete little poem:

> To see the Summer Sky
> Is Poetry, though never in a Book it lie —
> True Poems flee — [11]

Prospero responds to Ariel's song, his program for freedom, with a tone of personal regret and sadness, realizing that he, Prospero, will again be the loser:

> Why, that's my dainty Ariel! I shall miss thee;
> But yet thou shalt have freedom. So, so, so.
>
> (IV.i.95–6)

Ariel's last words in the play are a whispered aside: "Was't well done?" to which Prospero replies, "Bravely, my diligence. Thou shalt be free." (V.i.240–1) The limitless potential of the imagination has been harnessed in a shape and a form for a moment, but only for a moment.

Prospero himself has the very last words in the Epilogue, and they too dwell on freedom, though they speak more of death and despair. While Ariel, outside the limits of experience and deathless, goes to a freedom that is everything, Prospero, stripped of his powers and burdened by the known patterns of history, can go only back:

> Now I want
> Spirits to enforce, art to enchant;
> And my ending is despair
> Unless I be reliev'd by prayer,
> Which pierces so that it assaults
> Mercy itself, and frees all faults.
> As you from crimes would pardon'd be,
> Let your indulgence set me free.
>
> (Epilogue)

The Tempest is a sustained epiphany, like the kind of dream which moves through a long period of time and yet takes up only a few seconds of sleeping life. We are encouraged to see various aspects of human life in just the same relative way, suspending stasis beside flux.[12] When the play is finished and its dynamic forces have been collected in a state of immobility, we leave the magic island of art with a memory of its unchanging beauty, its control and imaginative resonance, and the memory is an initiation to many new and unending thoughts and reflections. Aesthetic finality is the prelude to a greater freedom for the life within the play, for now its components no longer exist in time nor in a narrative order which points towards their ending, but instead in a static pattern and an imaginative potential which none the less has the movement of a dance upon the yellow sands. In these teasing relativities, the heartbeat expanding outwards and contracting inwards, we find Shakespeare's most complete presentation of problems of time encountered in the "endless ending" of the romance experience. The paradoxes are Shakespeare's own, voiced in his language:

> Spring come to you at the farthest,
> In the very end of harvest!
> (IV.i.114–5)

We may return now to our initial question, what kind of play is *The Tempest*? One thing can be said with some confidence. This play, more perhaps than any other, leaves everything up to the observer by way of interpretation, concealing the author behind the artefact even when we may feel there are directly orphic comments. I am well aware that many critics see Prospero as God and Caliban as "congenitally vicious and incontinent",[13] while I have stressed the awkward, human fallibilities of the former and have perhaps sentimentalized the latter. The play as a whole elicits interpretations which range from the completely allegorical to a "rattling good yarn" response. Virtually every detail has been the subject of contradictory opinions. Nor can we really take the easy way out and say that *The Tempest* is ambiguous or ambivalent, since its own surface is so clear, controlled, and self-sufficient that it baffles a dualistic approach. However, it does draw out equally firm but contradictory feelings in every reader and audience, just as a storm will mean different things for the farmer, the sailor, and the holiday-maker. Although we attempt to find certainty in order to shore us against a potentially meaningless world, yet the qualities I have described in *The Tempest* should not be the cause of either fear or indignation. Rather, they should be acknowledged and celebrated for their rich mystery and wonder. After all, wonder, the normative response required by romances, is not a single thing for it depends upon the stimulus, and its presence depends equally upon the frame of mind of the perceiver. Such a statement should not be surprising to the reader of this book. Continually, in his many attempts to render the surface characteristics of romance, Shakespeare has been probing its sources, now taking the wonder for granted as an aesthetic and imaginative necessity, now challenging it with the rational mind, and now seeing it as the wilful creation of a person prepared to awaken a special kind of faith. *The Tempest*, by including amongst its personages a magician, evil rationalists, and an idealized adolescent woman, necessarily plays across the whole spectrum of these understandings, without overtly judging between them. It is amongst Shakespeare's greatest romances, and it is also his most consistent anti-romance. To say so is a humble admission of inadequacy in the presence of a consummate work of art which is as teasing as the Grecian urn.

Conclusion

In keeping with its argument, this book requires a conclusion which does not conclude. Despite the astonishing fertility of Shakespeare's creative mind and the diversity of his plays, he does appear to have been constantly preoccupied with a set of problems which are perhaps professional matters for every dramatist: how does one set about "conjuring" a group of people in a theatre to accept an imaginative fiction as "true"? And how does one provide an ending for a play which will leave a sense of completeness without forfeiting the artist's desire not to falsify the observation that life does not hold any complete endings, since after marriage there comes domestic life, and after death others will live on? No doubt there are many ways of describing Shakespeare's attempts to solve these problems, but by concentrating upon the material of romance we can, I feel, find descriptions which match the comprehensiveness of Shakespeare's plays (since romance itself is a wide-ranging mode of literature), and the immediate facts of literary history which place Elizabethan romance, and romance dramatized by Lyly, as central and inescapable influences upon Shakespeare. Time and again he drew from romance sources and the stock of romance motifs and attitudes, but always in a way that takes us into the essential nature of a genre rather than simply reproducing the dated conventions of the particular romances available to him. In doing so he may disturb, amuse, or reassure us, but in each case we are brought back to our own modes of perceiving the world around us and not simply to the contemplation of literature in its most fictive aspect. In the romance ending there is room for the "perfected bygone moments" of completeness as well as "the unfinished tide," and Lawrence is right to insist that both are possible in poetry as in life. The fact that discussion and argument about Shakespeare's endings, which are textually in existence and cannot whimsically be altered, will continue long after the present book is forgotten, is testimony to their multiplicity and to the endless possibilities of romance in the hands of a master dramatist.

APPENDIX

Elizabethan romance and stage comedy: historical survey

The relationship between Elizabethan romance and the romantic comedy of the 1590s is an extraordinarily difficult one to define, because of the diversity of the romance forms available. Here it is possible to give only a brief sketch, in order to provide a factual background to the ideas in this book.

The formation of Elizabethan prose romance

Elizabethan prose romance amalgamates many different forms. Hellenistic romances were revived and translated,[1] long medieval chivalric romances like the Arthurian stories, *Amadis de Gaule*,[2] *Palmerin of England*,[3] *Huon of Bordeaux*, and *Guy of Warwick*[4] enjoyed a continuous popularity, the second and third a result of the indefatigable efforts of translation of Antony Munday.[5] The poetic romances of Ariosto and Tasso were provoking acrimonious critical debate in Italy over the respectability of their literary pedigree, while the continental pastoral romances of Sannazzaro and Montemayor were important influences, ultimately stemming from Theocritus and Longus. The Italian *novella* of Boccaccio and Cinthio, drawing upon stories from the romance stock, were being imitated, for example by Bandello, whose works were themselves translated into French by Belleforest and into English (from the French) by Fenton and Painter. George Pettie's *Petite Palace of Pettie his Pleasure* draws mainly upon classical stories but presents them in the form of Italian *novelle*. There is, for example, a fundamental difference in setting. The Greek writers, Heliodorus and Achilles Tatius, and the writers of medieval, chivalric romances use travel over vast distances as a basic motif, whereas pastoral romance focusses upon a fixed, Arcadian locale, and Boccaccio sets most of his stories in the city. Elizabethan romances use all these settings from time to time, but there is an omnipresent courtly tone, even when the characters are in the pastoral landscape, a tone whose mode of expression is wit.

Elizabethan prose romance is a composite form, unifying the influences by a thematic concern with love, by a consistent tone of courtly sophistication, by examining the motives of characters more closely than had earlier forms of fiction, and by developing an interest in the morality of behavior. The two monuments of English prose romance are Lyly's *Euphues, The Anatomy of Wit*, published in 1578, and Sidney's *Arcadia*, known in its original manuscript form in the 1580s and published in the unfinished revised version in 1590. *Euphues* sustains a moral intensity that amounts to didacticism, with lengthy reflections and dialogues growing out of fairly slight Italianate incidents. The *Arcadia* manages to embed in the action itself an interest in the ethical status of motives and conduct, using the self-contained and sometimes dangerous world of Arcadian pastoral as the setting. Both works spawned many imitations, and the romances of Greene and Lodge straddle the period, showing the shift in taste from Euphuistic romance to Arcadian. By 1588, when Greene's *Perimedes the Blacksmith* and *Pandosto, The Triumph of Time* were published, Sidney's influence was predominant. The skill of Lyly, as G. K. Hunter points out, lies not in his originality but in his "unique skill in combining, balancing, and interrelating the various strands he inherited from others",[6] and in the case of Sidney too, traditional motifs are integrated and developed by a powerful mind, working within the Elizabethan preoccupation with emotional states and ethical problems.

The difference between prose and poetic romance in the Elizabethan age (the *Arcadia* and *The Faerie Queene*) is distinct, if difficult to formulate. There is a difference, for example, between the voice of the narrator in prose, confidential, persuasive, morally consistent — interested above all in telling a story that will keep the child from play and the old man from the chimney corner — and the generalizing allegorizing voice of the poet, perhaps less interested in what happens or even why it happens so much as what it means. We might point to a difference in verisimilitude, between the emotive and conceptual conviction which poetry must carry, set against the narrative continuity, psychological plausibility, and detailed explanatory commentary supplied by prose. Renaissance critics, by directing their attention primarily to the moral efficacy of literary works and their quality as artefacts, pay no attention to the distinction between poetry and prose. Sidney in his *Defence of Poetry* places both Xenophon and Heliodorus under the head of poets, for "it is not rhyming and versing that maketh a poet".[7]

The concentration in this book upon romances that end happily is a matter of convenience, since I have been comparing the genre with comedy. One could well speak in more detail than I have done of romance influence upon *Romeo and Juliet* and *Othello*, and list works that end tragically, such as those by Bandello, Belleforest, and Boccaccio and some by Greene. But that would be another subject. My emphasis is not in fact a serious distortion, because most Elizabethan prose romances do end happily. The optimistic vision of romance strives to turn the possibility of death and disaster into joy. Fortune, "after so sharpe a Catastrophe" is willing "to induce a comicall conclusion", and "tempers her storms with pleasant calms".[8]

Elizabethan literary romance and early dramatized romance

The early stages of the adaptation of romance into dramatic comedy are impossible to trace closely, because so many plays have been lost. In the lost plays written between 1570 and 1585, the link between romance and drama must have been close, judging from Barnaby Rich's comment in the. Conclusion to his set of short prose romances in *Rich's Farewell to Military Profession*:

> Gentle Reader, now thou hast perused these Histories to the ende, I doubte not but thou wilte deeme of them, as thei worthely deserue, and thinke suche vanities more fitter to bee presented on a Stage (as some of them haue been) then to bee published in Printe (as till now thei haue neuer been) . . . [9]

None of the plays to which Rich is referring has survived, and in fact we know he is lying when he says the stories have never been printed. Most are borrowed from Cinthio, Painter, and Pettie, and also to a lesser extent, from Gascoigne, Lyly, Udall, Golding, Underdowne, Belleforest, and Straparola.[10] Even so, his statement about drama reminds us of Stephen Gosson's comment that

> A *Palace of pleasure*, the *Golden Asse*, the *Æthiopian historie*, *Amadis of Fraunce*, the *Rounde table*, *baudie Comedies* in *Latine*, *French*, *Italian*, and *Spanish* haue beene throughly ransackt to furnish the Playe houses in London.[11]

This shows that forms of prose fiction — Greek romance, chivalric romance, and Italian *novella* — are adapted into Elizabethan prose romance and into dramatized romance. Amongst the titles of the lost plays, Greek romance is represented by *Chariclia* (1572), clearly based on Heliodorus's *Æthiopian History*, and the same play may have been revived in 1578 as *The Queen of Ethopia*. Chivalric romance lies behind titles like *Herpetulus the Blue Knight and Perobia* (1574), *The Red Knight* (1576), *The Irish Knight* (1577), *The Solitary Knight* (1577), and *The Knight in the Burning Rock* (1579). The *Amadis* cycles no doubt supply plots for *The Solitary Knight* and *Portio and Demorantes* (1580), while *Ariodante and Genevora* (1583) certainly told the same story as that in Canto V of *Orlando Furioso*, the tale later to be used as the basis for the Hero-Claudio plot in *Much Ado About Nothing*. *Cloridon and Radiamanta* (1572) may be the "Clodion and Bradamant" in Book xxxii of the *Orlando*, and *Panecia* (1574) may be Fenicia, whose story is told by Bandello and Belleforest.[12]

The few survivals of plays from the early period show some reasons for contemporary dismissal. *Common Conditions* is sustained by the pattern of separation-reunion-separation, and the writer assumes that, so long as there is an unrequited love affair, he needs no tight dramatic structure leading up to a climax. The story is said to be *"drawne out of the most famous historie of Galiarbus Duke of Arabia"*,[13] but no such story has been found. Greek romance is represented by the element of travel, chivalric romance by the cruel lord of an island who holds maidens captive,[14] and more generally by the ethic of

winning fame by doing brave deeds. The work is an unleave-
ned presentation of material from prose romance, episodic,
ill-adapted to the stage, and inadequately finished. *Clyomon
and Clamydes* is not much better. *Perceforest*, an anonymous
French prose romance of the fourteenth century, provides the
"leaues of worthy writers workes"[15] which are its source. Some
concern for the dramatic form is shown by the writer, since he
selects particular episodes instead of presenting the whole
story,[16] but there is little attempt to change or smooth out the
episodic quality of the original prose romance. The characters
berate fortune, like the narrators of prose romance, and the
problem of presenting supernatural forces on the stage is
crudely solved by introducing an allegorical *deus ex machina*,
Providence. The play is a series of abrupt parts rather than a
unified whole. The writer of *The Rare Triumphs of Love and
Fortune* goes further towards adapting the material into
dramatic form. His plot is constructed in such a way that we
constantly expect a marriage, and the central love interest is
not dissipated in loosely connected episodes. The device of
using a framing debate between the goddesses, Love and
Fortune, adds an overall interest to the romance plot, providing dramatic point and continuity, since the two goddesses
watch over the mortal love affair in order to test who is the
more powerful. The abstract formula, "love and fortune",
takes on a solid meaning when embodied in particular characters whom we see on the stage. The anonymous dramatist has
at least recognised that adaptation is necessary if romance is
to be placed successfully in the theatre.

There is a large gap in quality, if not in time, between these
plays and the dramatic output of John Lyly. His plays, written
between 1580 and 1590, thoroughly adapt romance motifs and
classical legends to the stage. Love is the dominant motivation
in each, wit is central to the dialogue, there are sub plots
intimately linked to the main action, and the romance incidents of disguise and the singing of songs are integrated.
Each play is a single action, planned and executed as a
dramatic piece, and the endings, while not always unequivocally festive, provide neat resolutions and climaxes,
towards which the action of each play builds. With Lyly's
plays, romantic comedy comes of age, no longer revealing its

narrative dependence upon prose romance and classical sources. His restrained, elegant, carefully patterned comedies are designed "to move inward delight, not outward lightnesse, and to breede (if it might bee) soft smiling, not loude laughing."[17] Robert Greene introduces into romantic comedy "a sure sense of homely values",[18] a special tone of courtesy and generosity, owing more to observation of life than to literary sources. Although Greene raises those questions about love identified by romance as important, and uses disguise, songs, and romance endings, his treatment is individual. Shakespeare's early comedies develop the genre to its limits of independence. Despite the dependence upon earlier romance of the plots in *The Two Gentlemen of Verona, A Midsummer Night's Dream, As You Like It,* and *Twelfth Night,* each play is a miracle of purely dramatic unity, in which romance motifs are absorbed, re-shaped, playfully challenged, and quickened into life on the stage.

The revival of romance on the stage, in the early seventeenth century, and the emergence of a kind of dramatized romance rather different from romantic comedy, has been briefly described on page 113. The relationship between romance and "citizen comedy" is even more complex. Although it is a topic that deserves a proper study, it is not relevant here.

Notes
Index

Notes

I *The sense of ending in Elizabethan romance*

1 Aristotle, *On the Art of Poetry*, chapter 7. Quoted from *Classical Literary Criticism*, translated T. S. Dorsch (Harmondsworth, 1965).

2 D. H. Lawrence, "Introduction to *New Poems*", reprinted in *Selected Literary Criticism: D. H. Lawrence*, ed. Anthony Beal (London, 1956), p. 85.

3 Chaucer, *Boece*, Book III, Prosa 8. Quotations from *The Works of Chaucer*, ed. F. N. Robinson, second edition (Oxford, 1957).

4 See Howard Felperin, *Shakespearean Romance* (Princeton, 1972), Part One. I am indebted to this book at various points in the present work. See also Hallett Smith, *Shakespeare's Romances* (San Marino, 1972).

5 The phrase has been given celebrity by Frank Kermode who entitled his book *The Sense of an Ending* (New York, 1967). His book is more general in its scope than literature alone. For an earlier account of some of the territory covered in the present book, see A. Thaler, "Shakespeare and the Unhappy Happy Ending". *PMLA*, xlii (1927), pp. 736–61.

6 Byron, *Don Juan*, Book III, Canto 9.

7 Chaucer, *Troilus and Criseyde*, V, lines 1807–9.

8 Rosemary Freeman, *The Faerie Queene: a companion for readers* (London, 1970), p. 37.

9 Sidney, *Old Arcadia*, ed. Jean Robertson (Oxford, 1973), p. 415.

10 Northrop Frye, *The Anatomy of Criticism* (Princeton, 1957), pp. 186–7. All writers on romance and comedy are deeply indebted to Frye for establishing these genres as matters for serious analysis: see especially *A Natural Perspective* (New York, 1965) and more recently *Secular Scripture: study of the structure of Romance* (Harvard, 1980). However, the critical stance in the present book is much more based on the detail of particular texts than are Frye's works, and although his influence is pervasive, it is difficult to acknowledge in specifics.

11 *Forbonius and Prisceria* (1584); Bodleian, Tanner 220, sig. K3 r.

12 For a compressed account of this complex matter, see the footnote to Chaucer's "The Knight's Tale" in Robinson's edition, p. 675.

13 *Clyomon and Clamydes* (published 1599 but certainly performed at least a decade earlier); Malone Society Reprint, ed. W. W. Greg (Oxford, 1913). sig, D2 v. A modern edition is given by B. J. Littleton (The Hague, 1968).

14 Sig. Gl v.

15 *Twelfth Night*, II.ii, lines 38–9. All quotations from Shakespeare are taken from the Alexander text (London, 1951).

16 Sidney, *Old Arcadia*, p. 415.

17 *Ibid.*

18 p. 416.

19 *King Lear*, I.ii.128.

20 Greene, *Pandosto. Life and Complete Works of Robert Greene*, ed. A. B. Grosart (London, 1881–6) in 15 volumes, IV, p. 315.

21 *Ibid.*

22 Stephen Gosson, *Plays Confuted in Five Actions* (1582). Bodleian, Malone 476, sig. C6 r.

23 E.g., *Havelok the Dane* and *Sir Eglamour of Artois*. See J. J. O'Connor, *Amadis de Gaule and its influence on Elizabethan literature* (New Brunswick, 1970), pp. 17–18, and Mary Patchell, *The 'Palmerin' Romances in Elizabethan Prose Fiction* (New York, 1947), p. 28.

24 Barnabe Rich, *Riche his Farewell to Military Profession* (1581). Bodleian, Tanner 213, sig. Dd2 r.

25 See S. L. Wolff, *The Greek Romances in Elizabethan Prose Fiction* (New York, 1912), p. 183.

26 Sidney, *Old Arcadia*, p. 403.

27 p. 410.

28 p. 412.

29 p. 414.

30 p. 415.

31 Lyly, *Euphues and His England. Complete Works of John Lyly*, ed. R. W. Bond (Oxford, 1902) in 3 volumes, II, p. 228.

32 Sidney, *Old Arcadia*, p. 417.

33 Variorum Edition of Plays of W. B. Yeats, ed. R. K. Alspach (London, 1966), p. 1049. Cf. Kent, "He'll shape his old course in a country new", *King Lear*, I.i.187.

34 *A Hundredth Sundry Flowres* (1573), Bodleian, Wood 329, sig. M2 r.

35 Spenser, *The Faerie Queene*, VII.viii.2. All quotations from the edition by J. C. Smith and E. de Selincourt, *Spenser: Poetical Works* (Oxford, 1912).

36 VII.vii.12.

II *The sense of an ending in early Elizabethan romantic comedy*

1 F. P. Wilson, *The English Drama, 1485–1585*, ed. G. K. Hunter (Oxford, 1969), p. 115.

2 For some information on the lost plays, consult *Annals of English Drama, 975–1700* by Alfred Harbage, revised by S. Schoenbaum (London, 1964).

3 Stephen Gosson, *Plays Confuted in Five Actions* (1582). Bodleian, Malone 476, sig. D5 v.

4 G. K. Hunter, *John Lyly: the humanist as courtier* (London, 1962), p. 204. I am generally indebted to this book, especially Chapter VI, "Lyly and Shakespeare".

5 Malone Society Reprint, ed. W. W. Greg (Oxford, 1930), line 1812.

6 It is not certain that this play is pre-Shakespearean. As R. W. Bond says, "The date is harder to fix than that of any other play of Lyly": *Works*, III, p 295. Bond concludes that it was produced in 1586–8 and revived in 1599 or 1600. The play is characteristic of Lyly's dramatized romance, and this is perhaps the only relevant fact for my purposes.

7 Lyly, *Gallathea*, II.ii.5–8. *Works*, II, p. 441.

8 C. L. Barber, *Shakespeare's Festive Comedy* (Princeton, 1959).

9 *Gallathea*, V.iii.142–3. *Works*, II, 470.

10 This is the play used by Barber as his prototype for "festive comedy". My disagreements with Barber's overall argument do not prevent my deep admiration for his pioneering work, for without it one would have difficulty in persuading even literary critics that romantic comedy is a mode which invites the full rigors of literary and historical scholarship. He helped to put the subject on the map, and his interpretations of individual plays are still amongst the best we have.

11 *James the Fourth*, V.vi.173–4. Quoted from the New Mermaids edition, ed. J. A. Lavin (London, 1967). (Note that *king* is emended to *kind*)

12 *Friar Bacon and Friar Bungay*, Scene xvi, lines 38–9. New Mermaids edition, ed. J. A. Lavin (London, 1967).

13 Scene xiv, lines 81–92.

14 Scene xiv, lines 93–7.

15 *James the Fourth*, V.vi.234–5. For sensitive and helpful explorations of the nature of Greene's comedy, see Una Ellis-Fermor, "Marlowe and Greene: a note on their relations as dramatic artists" in *Studies in Honor of T. W. Baldwin*, ed. D. C. Allen (Urbana, 1958), and Norman Sanders, "The Comedy of

Greene and Shakespeare" in *Early Shakespeare*, Stratford upon Avon Studies, iii (1961).

16   The critic who makes this point strongly is Stanley Wells in "Shakespeare and Romance" in *Later Shakespeare*, Stratford upon Avon Studies, viii (1966). This brief but illuminating essay is still generally valuable.

17   See Wolff (*passim*).

18   Geoffrey Bullough, *Narrative and Dramatic Sources of Shakespeare* (8 volumes), I (London, 1977), pp. 9–11. See also R. A. Foakes's Arden edition of the play (London, 1962), Introduction.

19   Bullough, I, 10.

20   *Ibid.*

21   For information on the sources see Bullough, I; Clifford Leech's Introduction to the Arden edition (London, 1969); and Introduction to Judith M. Kennedy's edition of *George of Montemayor's Diana . . .* (Oxford, 1968).

22   Harold F. Brooks, "Two Clowns in a Comedy (to say nothing of the Dog): Launce (and Crab) in *The Two Gentlemen of Verona*", *Essays and Studies 1963* (London, 1963), pp. 91–100.

23   R. G. Hunter, *Shakespeare and the Comedy of Forgiveness* (New York, 1965). See also the valuable interpretations in Ralph Berry, *Shakespeare's Comedies* (Princeton, 1972); Inga-Stina Ewbank, "'Were man but constant, he were perfect': Constancy and Consistency in *The Two Gentlemen of Verona*" in *Shakespearean Comedy*, Stratford upon Avon Studies, xiv (1972); and Alexander Leggatt, *Shakespeare's Comedy of Love* (London, 1974).

24   *George of Montemayor's Diana*, ed. Kennedy, p. 241.

25   See Berry, *Shakespeare's Comedies*.

26   *The Old Wives' Tale*, Scolar Press facsimile, sigs F3 v and r.

III   *Shakespeare's mature romantic comedies*

1   Almost all modern critics stress the significance of this moment, but see especially Bobbyan Roesen, who demonstrates how the dénouement is carefully prepared for by muted references to death: *Love's Labour's Lost*", *Shakespeare Quarterly*, iv (1953), pp. 411–26. More generally on the play, I should like to say I have found the following accounts helpful: Ralph Berry, "The Words of Mercury", *Shakespeare Survey*, xxii (1969), pp. 69–77; J. L. Calderwood, *"Love's Labour's Lost:* a wantoning with words", *Studies in English Literature*, v (1965), pp. 317–32; J. V. Cunningham, "With That Facility: false starts and revisions in *Love's Labour's Lost*" in *Essays on Shakespeare* (Princeton, 1965);

Philip Edwards, *Shakespeare and the Confines of Art* (London, 1968); Inga-Stina Ewbank, "'These Pretty Devices': a study of masques in plays" in *A Book of Masques*, ed. T. J. B. Spencer (Cambridge, 1967).

2   Leggatt: "The enclosed world of courtship is attacked from two sides at once. A new life begins in Jaquenetta's belly, and an old life ends somewhere in France: courtship is only a moment in a larger cycle." *Shakespeare's Comedy of Love*, p. 83.

3   Malory, *Le Morte d'Arthur*, Book IV, Chapter 19.

4   *The Parliament of Fowls*, lines 660–1.

5   *The Faerie Queene*, I.xii.41.

6   Barber, p. 117: "The only syntax that matters is 'When . . . Then . . .'" There is a considerable literature on the Songs, but see especially Cyrus Hoy, *The Hyacinth Room* (London, 1964), pp. 36–8: C. M. McClay, "The Dialogues of Spring and Winter: a key to the unity of *Love's Labour's Lost*," *Shakespeare Quarterly*, xviii (1967), pp. 119–27.

7   Aristotle, *op. cit.* At this point I might mention that my understanding of *The Dream* has been enhanced by the following critical accounts: J. L. Calderwood, "*A Midsummer Night's Dream* and the Illusion of Drama", *Modern Language Quarterly*, xxvi (1965), pp. 506–22; G. K. Hunter, *Shakespeare: The Later Comedies*, Writers and Their Works, p. 143 (London, 1962); P. A. Olson, "*A Midsummer Night's Dream* and the meaning of Court Marriage". *English Literary History*, xxiv (1957), pp. 95–119; Norman Rabkin, *Shakespeare and the Common Understanding* (New York, 1967); M. Taylor, "The Darker Purpose of *A Midsummer Night's Dream*", *Studies in English Literature*, ix (1969), pp. 259–73 and (especially) D. P. Young, *Something of Great Constancy: the art of 'A Midsummer Night's Dream'* (New Haven, 1966).

8   *The Old Wives' Tale*, sig. B2 v. Northrop Frye uses the quotation in his discussion of conventions of comedy and romance in *A Natural Perspective*, p. 13.

9   *Twelfth Night*, V.i.360.

10 See, for example, Sigurd Burckhardt, *Shakespearean Meanings* (Princeton, 1968) and J. R. Brown, *Shakespeare and his Comedies* (London, 1962), as well as the balanced account of these issues in Leggatt.

11 James Smith, *Shakespearian and Other Essays* (Cambridge, 1974), pp. 43–68 *passim*. I find all of Smith's essays on the comedies very impressive, since they show that we do not *need* to follow Frye in order to be rigorous!

12 Anne Barton, "*As You Like It* and *Twelfth Night*: Shakespeare's sense of an ending", *Shakespearian Comedy*, Stratford upon Avon

Studies, xiv (1972). As the title implies, I am indebted to this essay, as well as to D. P. Young, *The Heart's Forest: a study of Shakespeare's pastoral plays* (New Haven, 1972); R. P. Draper, "Shakespeare's Pastoral Comedy", *Etudes Anglaises*, xi (1958), pp. 1–17; S. Barnet, "'Strange Events': improbability in *As You Like It*", *Shakespeare Studies*, iv (1968), pp. 119–31; H. Jenkins, "*As You Like It*", *Shakespeare Survey*, viii (1955), pp. 40–51; M. Mincoff, "What Shakespeare did to *Rosalynde*", *Shakespeare Jahrbuch*, xcvi (1960), pp. 78–89; John Shaw, "Fortune and Nature in *As You Like It*", *Shakespeare Quarterly*, vi (1955), pp. 49–50.

13 Lodge, *Rosalynde* (1592), Scolar Press facsimile, sig. M3 r.

14 sig. M1 r.

15 Spenser, *Epithalamion*, lines 389–408.

16 See Young, *The Heart's Forest*, pp. 46–50 and M. S. Kuhn, "Much Virtue in *If*," *Shakespeare Quarterly*, xviii (1977), pp. 40–50. Kuhn compares the practice of Sidney, and concludes that "*As You Like It* is a series of inspired improvisations in the key of *If*."

17 Barbara Everett, "*Much Ado About Nothing*", *Critical Quarterly*, iii (1961), pp. 319–35, perhaps the best piece on the play. See also the fine essays by James Smith (above) and A. P. Rossiter, *Angel With Horns* (London, 1961).

18 See Bullough, *Narrative and Dramatic Sources of Shakespeare* II; C. T. Prouty, *The Sources of "Much Ado About Nothing"* (New Haven, 1950) and L. G. Salingar, *Shakespeare and the Traditions of Comedy* (Cambridge, 1974), pp. 298–325 *passim*.

19 Rich, *Farewell*, sig. L4 r.

20 Sig. M1 r.

21 I have found the following pieces full of insight on *Twelfth Night:* Hunter, *The Later Comedies;* Harold Jenkins, "Shakespeare's *Twelfth Night*", *Rice Institute Pamphlets*, xlv (1959); Clifford Leech, *Twelfth Night and the Design of Shakespearian Comedy* (Toronto, 1968); L. G. Salingar, "The Design of *Twelfth Night*", *Shakespeare Quarterly*, ix (1958), pp. 117–39.

22 I am reassured to find my harsh criticism of Sir Toby supported independently by Ralph Berry in "*Twelfth Night*: the experience of the audience", *Shakespeare Survey* 34 (1981), pp. 111–20.

IV *The "problem" comedies*

1 *Annals of English Drama* place the limits for *All's Well* as *c.* 1601–04, and for *Measure for Measure* as *c.* 1603–04. The tendency of

my argument in this chapter is that the former is more structurally innovative, but this does not prove anything.

2   Fletcher, *The Faithful Shepherdess*, To the Reader": "A tragi-comedy is not so called in respect of mirth and killing, but in respect it wants deaths . . ." The Renaissance "theories" of tragi-comedy are surveyed in M. Doran, *Endeavours of Art* (Madison, 1954); M. T. Herrick, *Comic Theory in the Sixteenth Century* (Urbana, 1950); and B. Weinberg, *A History of Literary Criticism in the Italian Renaissance* in two volumes (Chicago, 1961). Although it is not specifically the tragi-comic which interests me in this chapter, it is fair to remind the reader of the works on the subject such as W. W. Armstrong, *Shakespeare's Problem Comedies* (New York, 1960 and Ernest Schanzer, *The Problem Plays of Shakespeare* (New York, 1963).

3   G. K. Hunter (ed.) Arden edition of *All's Well That Ends Well* (London, 1959), p. lv. An honorable exception is Felperin: "The problem plays stand midway between the romantic comedies and the romances in more than a chronological sense . . ." *Shakespearean Romance* (above), p. 96.

4   Shakespeare shows himself equally capable of using Boccaccio to write a different kind of play, in *Cymbeline* (see below).

5   Salingar, *Shakespeare and the Traditions of Comedy*.

6   Lever edits the Arden edition of the Play (London, 1965) while Wilson Knight's essay appears in *The Wheel of Fire* (London, 1949).

7   Harriet Hawkins, "'The Devil's Party': virtues and vices in *Measure for Measure*", *Shakespeare Survey*, xxxi (1978). J. C. Maxwell, *Measure for Measure*: the play and the themes", *Proceedings of the British Academy*, lx (1974). An interesting essay on the play, which anticipates some of my own argument, is in Ralph Berry's *Shakespearean Structures* (London, 1981): "Hierarchic Forms: language and structure in *Measure for Measure*".

8   Peter Ure, *Shakespeare: The Problem Plays*, Writers and their works, 140 (Harlow, 1964), p. 19.

9   II.ii.59–63. Isabella here denies that "ceremony" is as powerful as "mercy" in the ruler's repertoire, but she is arguing *against* the ruler himself.

10 In raising this possibility I am, with some apprehensiveness, going against the opinion of J. C. Maxwell (p. 19), since he believes that Isabella and the audience have nothing to fear at this stage. I believe that it is important to note that, although we are not encouraged totally to mistrust the Duke's good intentions, yet he has shown bad judgement on occasions, he

has lied (callously) to Isabella about her brother's life, and anyway the action is not firmly in his own hands yet, since he has already been overruled by Angelo when the reprieve did not come. Furthermore, the Duke at this moment is at his most inscrutably ambiguous, and although we *hope* he will act benevolently, yet his actions do not immediately inspire confidence, especially since one of the play's dominant messages is that a person is most likely to act differently when he wears a uniform. It is surely crucial to the dramatic effect in this scene that everybody is kept in a state of suspense about what the Duke will do, and we cannot so easily be certain that "All is going according to plan so far" (Maxwell).

11 See the description of the reconciliation in the *Old Arcadia*, p. 278.
12 Hazlitt, *Characters of Shakespeare's Plays* (1817). *Complete Works of William Hazlitt*, ed. P. P. Howe (London, 1930), IV, p. 346.
13 A. P. Rossiter, *Angel With Horns* (London, 1961), p. 168.
14 *The Winter's Tale*, V.i.151–2.
15 *The Tempest*, V.i.65.
16 Although *All's Well* has been widely neglected, it has inspired some very fine commentary, and I am deeply indebted to the following: *"All's Well That Ends Well:* Shakespeare's Play of Endings" by Ian Donaldson, *Essays in Criticism*, xxvii (1977), pp. 34–55; Barbara Everett's Introduction to the New Penguin edition of the play (Harmondsworth, 1970), and Wilson Knight's essay in *The Sovereign Flower* (London, 1958). See also Jay L. Halio, *"All's Well That Ends Well"*, *Shakespeare Quarterly* xv (1964), pp. 33–43.
17 For the surprisingly few examples of the bed trick on the stage before the "problem" plays, see W. R. Bowden, "The Bed-Trick, 1604–42 . . .", *Shakespeare Studies*, v (1969), pp. 112–23, and T. S. Dorsch, *"Measure for Measure* and its Contemporary Audience," *Shakespeare Jahrbuch*, cxiv (1978–9), pp. 202–16. On the available evidence, it is even possible to argue that Shakespeare was the first to make significant use of the device, although it is, of course, very common in earlier prose romance and Italian tales.
18 For textual detail, see Richard A. Levin, "The two French Lords of *All's Well That Ends Well"*, *Notes and Queries*, xxvi (1979), pp. 122–5.
19 See Christopher Hill, *Milton and the English Revolution* (1977).
20 Francis Meres, *Palladis Tamia* (1958). Meres was speaking of Shakespeare's non-dramatic poetry, but it can be assumed that he is summing up a more comprehensive impression of Shakespeare's writings.

V *Romance in the tragedies*

1   The influence of the Italian tale on these plays is analyzed by
    L. G. Salingar in *Shakespeare and the Traditions of Comedy*,
    Chapter 6. While I believe that Salingar's preoccupation with
    Italian backgrounds underestimates the importance of English
    romance, he certainly provides us with a wealth of information.

2   See, for example, *As You Like It*, IV.i.83–95 where Rosalind
    asserts that the stories are all "lies", and *Much Ado About
    Nothing*, V.ii.31, where Benedick is similarly satirical.

3   I refrain from citing examples of this tendency, but am happy to
    acknowledge some critics who treat Cressida with sympathy:
    Carolyn Asp, "In Defense of Cressida," *Studies in Philology*, lxxiv
    (1977), pp. 406–17; John Bayley, *The Uses of Division: Unity and
    Disharmony in Literature* (London, 1976); Gayle Greene,
    "Shakespeare's Cressida: 'a kind of self'" in *The Woman's Part:
    feminist criticism of Shakespeare*, ed. C. R. S. Lenz and others
    (Urbana, 1980).

4   "Romance in *King Lear*", *English* (1978), pp. 5–21. See also
    Felperin, *Shakespearean Romance*, Chapter 4. I should mention
    also the various, stimulating essays linking *Lear* with the
    pastoral: David Young, *The Heart's Forest;* Maynard Mack, *King
    Lear in Our Time* (Berkeley, 1965); Rosalie Colie, *Shakespeare's
    Living Art* (Princeton, 1974).

5   J. C. Maxwell, "The Technique of Invocation in *King Lear*",
    Modern Language Review, xlv (1950), p. 142.

6   Barbara Everett succinctly examines some of the assumptions,
    whether pessimistic or optimistic, which have been held from
    Johnson to recent times, in "The New *King Lear*", *Critical
    Quarterly*, ii (1960), pp. 325–39.

7   It should be mentioned in passing that the Quarto text gives
    these lines to "Duke", who may be Albany. This would not
    change my point, since it is the attitude itself which matters.

8   For the fullest presentation of the sources, see Bullough,
    Narrative and Dramatic Sources of Shakespeare, vii (1973).

9   See Everett, "The New King Lear", pp. 332–4, discussing this
    issue.

10 "Society, as we have constituted it, will have no place for me,
    has none to offer; but Nature, whose sweet rains fall on unjust
    and just alike, will have clefts in the rocks where I may hide,
    and secret valleys in whose silence I may weep undisturbed.
    She will hang the night with stars so that I may walk abroad in
    the darkness without stumbling, and send the wind over my
    footprints so that none may track me to my hurt: she will

cleanse me in great waters, and with bitter herbs make me whole."

11 Walter C. Foreman, Jr., *The Music of the Close: final scenes of Shakespeare's tragedies* (Kentucky, 1978).

12 Quoted by Foreman on p. 179 from Langer, *Feeling and Form* (New York, 1953), p. 334.

13 Foreman's formulation may be of interest here:

"The subjunctive is, in a sense, Cleopatra's proper mood, and as we get farther into the scene, into the 'play' she is putting on, her 'subjunctive' will seem increasingly to be 'indicative', which is like drama itself — the subjunctive pretending to be the indicative, an imaginary world presenting itself to us as if it were 'real'." (p. 185)

14 In Book x of *The Republic*, the comments which have stung so many poets into writing "Defenses" of imaginative literature.

15 Sidney, *A Defence of Poetry: miscellaneous prose of Sir Philip Sidney*, ed. K. Duncan-Jones and J. van Dorsten (Oxford, 1973), p. 78.

16 See Katherina's "the moon changes even as your mind" in *The Taming of the Shrew*, IV.v.20. Cf. Orlando's "I can live no longer by thinking" in *As You Like It*, V.ii.47, which emphasizes the amount of "counterfeiting" and creating a new reality which has been practiced in the Forest of Arden up to this moment.

17 G. Wilson Knight, *The Crown of Life* (London, 1947), p. 34.

18 This is one possible interpretation of the facts given by G. F. Reynolds in "*Mucedorus*, Most Popular Elizabethan Play?" in *Studies in the English Renaissance Drama*, ed. J. W. Bennett and others (London, 1961), pp. 248–69.

19 Like most non-Shakespearean romance, the plays of this period have not attracted thorough, critical studies, but see J. F. Danby, *Poets on Fortune's Hill* (London, 1952); W. Creizenach's still excellent study of the whole period, *The English Drama in the Age of Shakespeare* (London, 1916), the only portion translated from this monumental study; E. Waith, *The Pattern of Tragicomedy in Beaumont and Fletcher* (New Haven, 1952); and the introductions to the various modern, scholarly editions of texts. It is a field in need of attention.

20 See especially the interesting discussion by Una Ellis-Fermor in *The Jacobean Drama*, (fourth edition, London, 1958), Chapter xi, where she argues for a special "mood" of tragi-comedy, which is homogeneous and distinct from the other genres. For more detail on the revival of romance in the Jacobean period, see Fitzroy Pyle, *The Winter's Tale: a commentary on the structure* (London, 1969), pp. 171 ff.

VI   *Shakespeare's romances*

1   *A Defence of Poetry, Miscellaneous Prose of Sir Philip Sidney,* ed. K. Duncan-Jones and J. van Dorsten (Oxford, 1973), p. 113.

2   Whetstone, Dedication to *Promos and Cassandra* (1578).

3   Gosson, *Plays Confuted* (1578).

4   As for all plays, the most thorough presentation of sources and analogues for *Pericles* comes in Geoffrey Bullough's monumental *Narrative and Dramatic Sources of Shakespeare,* vi (1966). See also the scholarly introductions to the Arden and New Cambridge editions, edited by F. D. Hoeniger and J. C. Maxwell respectively. Also generally relevant to the material in this chapter are the treatments by Hallett Smith in *Shakespeare's Romances* (San Marino, 1972), Carol Gesner, *Shakespeare and the Greek Romances: A study of origins* (Kentucky, 1970), and Felperin. Because my concentration is upon romance itself, it is not necessary here to attend to Felperin's interesting argument about medieval, morality traditions behind *Pericles* in "Shakespeare's Miracle Play", *Shakespeare's Quarterly* 18 (1967), pp. 363–74.

5   See the discussions in Bullough, Hoeniger, and Maxwell.

6   Sidney, *New Arcadia,* p. 483.

7   Wilson Knight points out the echo from *Twelfth Night* in *The Crown of Life,* p. 65. It is interesting to note in this context the similarities between *Pericles* and Chaucer's "Man of Law's Tale", a connection mentioned but not developed by Ann Thompson in *Shakespeare's Chaucer* (Liverpool, 1978), pp. 83–4. They cannot be explained merely as the result of a shared source.

8   General reference could be made here to D. W. Harding, "Shakespeare's Final View of Women", *Times Literary Supplenent,* (1979), pp. 59–61; and C. L. Barber, "'Thou that beget'st him that did thee beget': Transformation in *Pericles* and *The Winter's Tale*", *Shakespeare Survey,* 22 (1969), pp. 59–67.

9   But it was highly popular in its own day. The vogue of such a "mouldy tale" is what seems to have irked Ben Jonson. Judging from recent performances in England by the Prospect Theatre Company and the Royal Shakespeare Company, there is no reason why *Pericles* cannot be popular again with audiences. Perhaps it is really the critics who are unsympathetic, with some exceptions such as John Arthos, *"Pericles, Prince of Tyre:* A Study in the Dramatic Use of Romantic Narrative", *Shakespeare Quarterly,* iv (1953), and of course Wilson Knight, whose essays in *The Crown of Life* on all these plays have a vibrant respect.

Knight has the wonderfully generous capacity to make the very most of every play.

10 See *The Crown of Life*, where Knight sees the last plays as an "apocalypse" which "radiates out first into *Cymbeline*", p. 202.

11 For discussion and references, see the introductions to the Arden edition (James Nosworthy) and the New Cambridge edition (J. C. Maxwell).

12 C. B. Young, "The Stage History of *Cymbeline*" in the New Cambridge edition (Cambridge, 1960), p. liii. Shaw's own caustic and illuminating remarks on the play are conveniently printed in *Shaw on Shakespeare*, ed. Edwin Wilson (Harmondsworth, 1969).

13 Sidney, *New Arcadia*, p. 444. Alan Brissenden remarks in private correspondence that the parallels were noticed in a research seminar at Adelaide University recently, so perhaps the idea has more currency than I thought when I first wrote this book.

14 Sidney, *New Arcadia*, p. 387.

15 p. 322.

16 p. 573. To mention one more similarity between *Cymbeline* and the *New Arcadia*, compare the rhetoric used by Pyrocles before the "headlines" Philoclea (pp. 564–5) with Imogen's lament over the headless body in IV.ii.

17 See Emrys Jones, "Stuart *Cymbeline*", *Essays in Criticism*, xi (1961), pp. 84–99, and J. P. Brockbank, "History and Histrionics in *Cymbeline*", *Shakespeare Survey*, xi (1958), pp. 42–9.

18 See James Nosworthy in his Introduction to the Arden *Cymbeline* (London, 1955), Section 10. See also F. D. Hoeninger, "Irony and Romance in *Cymbeline*", *Studies in English Literature*, ii (1962), pp. 219–28.

19 Nosworthy, Section 11. Nosworthy wisely does not attempt to categorize the play too closely: "It is not just one or the other of these things but all of them, and with something else besides." He makes an interesting allusion to the late Beethoven who "displays the same arbitrary dispersal of material as we find in *Cymbeline*".

20 Quoted from Bullough, vii. p. 156.

21 p. 176.

22 p. 199.

23 There have been some fine pieces written on *The Winter's Tale* and some are relevant here: Wilson Knight's chapter in *The Crown of Life*; Inga-Stina Ewbank, "The Triumph of Time in *The Winter's Tale*", *Review of English Literature*, v (1964), pp. 83–100; John Lawlor, "*Pandosto* and the Nature of Dramatic Romance", *Philological Quarterly*, xli (1962), pp. 96–113; L. G.

Salingar, "Time and Art in Shakespeare's Romances", *Renaissance Drama*, ix (1966), pp. 3–35; D. P. Young's chapter in *The Heart's Forest* (above); Ralph Berry, *"The Winter's Tale*: A Dance to the Music of Time" in *Shakespearean Structures*; Rosalie Colie, *Shakespeare's "Living Art"* (Princeton, 1974), Chapters 6 and 7.

24 An interesting discussion of Leontes' psychological dimension is given by Joan Hartwig in *Shakespeare's Tragicomic Vision* (Louisiana, 1972). She argues that the psychological power is modified by comic elements.

25 Francis Berry, *The Shakespearean Inset* (London, 1965), p. 93.

26 See e.g., J. H. P. Pafford, ed. Arden edition (London, 1963), pp. lxi–lxii. On the Gentleman's language see Nevill Coghill, "Six Points of Stage-Craft in *The Winter's Tale,*" *Shakespeare Survey*, 11 (1958), pp. 38–9.

27 It may surprise some to know that the final scene is actually shorter in number of words than the scene between the Gentlemen (V.i), a fact which the memory might falsify. It is not to say the final scene will necessarily be quicker in performance time, however.

28 *Paradise Lost*, xii, lines 552–6.

29 Epilogue to *As You Like It*.

30 There are many theoretical works on the subject of time in Shakespeare, which are generally relevant to the discussion in this book. A convenient bibliography can be found in Wylie Sypher's *The Ethic of Time: Structures of Experience in Shakespeare* (New York, 1967), and it is necessary also to single out the following: Tom Driver, *The Sense of History in Greek and Shakespearean Drama* (New York, 1960); Douglas L. Peterson, *Time, Tide and Tempest: A Study of Shakespeare's Romances* (California, 1973), and Frederick Turner, *Shakespeare and the Nature of Time* (New York, 1971). A related book which I have found most stimulating was recommended to me by John McGahern: Paolo Vivante, *The Homeric Imagination* (Indiana, 1970).

VII   *The Tempest*

1 Henry James, "The Tempest", reprinted in *Henry James: Selected Criticism*, ed. Morris Shapiro (London, 1963).

2 See Wells, "Shakespeare and Romance".

3 Carol Gesner, *Shakespeare and the Greek Romances* (above); the same author's *"The Tempest* as Pastoral Romance", *Shakespeare Quarterly*, x (1959), pp. 531–39; see also Young's *The Heart's Forest*.

4   See Bullough viii and the Introduction to Frank Kermode's Arden edition of *The Tempest* (1954). D. P. Young in *The Heart's Forest* emphasizes the background of the *commedia dell'arte*, drawing upon K. M. Lea's *Italian Popular Comedy*, 2 vols. (Oxford, 1934). James Smith's essay in *Shakespearian and Other Essays* (above) is an interesting attempt to make a literary interpretation of the existence of sources in travel literature, and Enid Welsford writes on the importance of the masque in *The Court Masque* (Cambridge, 1927). See also J. M. Nosworthy, "The Narrative Sources of *The Tempest*", *Review of English Studies*, xxiv (1948), pp. 281–94, which adds *The Aeneid* to the growing pool of sources.

5   I owe this perception to Jane Whiteley. Only a small sample of verbal and thematic reminiscences can be given in a short footnote, and the examples are taken from *King Lear* only:
I.i.6 Blow, till thou burst thy wind, if room enough!
Lear III.ii.1 Blow, winds, and crack your cheeks! . . .

II.ii.1 All the infections that the sun sucks up
        From bogs, fens, flats . . .
Lear II.iv.165 You fen-suck'd fogs, . . .

IV.i.182 the filthy-mantled pool
Lear III.iv.130 the green mantle of the standing pool;

V.i.45–6 . . . and rifted Jove's stout oak / With his own bolt;
Lear III.ii.5 Vaunt-couriers to oak-cleaving thunderbolts, . . .

V.i.197 But, O, how oddly will it sound that I
        Must ask my child forgiveness!
Lear V.iii.10 When thou dost ask me blessing, I'll kneel down,
        And ask of thee forgiveness:

V.i.240 And were brought moping hither.
Lear Iv.vi.179 . . . we came crying hither:

6   I have not done a thorough count, but I would guess that there is at least as large a proportion of passages which end in a half- line in this play as in any other by Shakespeare. This characteristic might have a lot to do with the cumulative effect of the play, with its haunting sea music. For a more specifically imagistic study, see Reuben Brower's stimulating essay in *The Fields of Light* (New York, 1951).

7   Keats's sonnet "On the Sea" was inspired by a line which he slightly misremembers from *King Lear*: " . . . the passage in Lear — 'Do you not hear the sea', — has haunted me intensely"; but there are echoes of *The Tempest* as well. Quotation from letter to Reynolds, 17–18 April, 1817.

8   Yeats, "A Prayer for my Daughter".

9   *W. H. Auden, Collected Longer Poems* (London, 1968), p. 212.

10   See Felperin, *Shakespearean Romance*, p. 276.

11   *The Complete Poems of Emily Dickinson*, ed. T. H. Johnson (London, 1970), p. 623.

12   See the suggestive comments about "cycle" and "crisis" in the last plays by Clifford Leech in "The Structure of the Last Plays", *Shakespeare Survey*, 11 (1958), pp. 19–30, a concept which is important to my discussion though I use different terms. I might mention that I am also generally indebted in this chapter to the fine section on *The Tempest* in Michael Goldman's *Shakespeare and the Energies of Drama* (Princeton, 1972).

13   Felperin, *Shakespearean Romance*, p. 263.

Appendix

1   See Wolff.

2   See O'Connor.

3   See Patchell.

4   R. S. Crane, "The Vogue of *Guy of Warwick* from the close of the Middle Ages to the Romantic Revival", *PMLA*, xxx (1915), pp. 125–94.

5   G. R. Hayes, "Anthony Munday's Romances of Chivalry", *The Library*, 4th series, vi (1926), pp. 57–81 and vii (1927), pp. 31–8.

6   Hunter, *Lyly*, p. 258.

7   *Miscellaneous Prose*, p. 81.

8   *Perimedes the Blacksmith* (1588), Greene, *Works*, vii. 51.

9   B. Rich, *Rich's Farewell to Military Profession* (1581), Bodleian, Tanner, 213, sig. Dd3 v. Reproduced in facsimile, ed. T. M. Cranfill (Austin, 1959).

10   Cranfill, "Introduction", pp.xvii–xxxvi.

11   S. Gosson, *Plays Confuted in Five Actions* (1582), Bodleian, Malone 476, sig. D5 v.

12   Information in this paragraph comes from W. Creizenach, *The English Drama in the Age of Shakespeare* (1918), L. M. Ellison, *The Early Romantic Drama at the English Court* (Menasha, 1917), and A. Harbage, *Annals of English Drama*, revised S. Schoenbaum (1964).

13   *Common Conditions* (1576), title page. Facsimile ed. by Tucker Brooke (1915).

14   Noted by Creizenach, p. 19.

15 *Clyomon and Clamydes* (1599), title page. Malone Society Reprint, ed. W. W. Greg (Oxford, 1913). The date of performance is certainly earlier than 1599: 1570–83).

16 This point is made by B. J. Littleton (ed.), *Clyomon and Clamydes* (The Hague and Paris, 1968), p. 39.

17 Prologue to *Sapho and Phao*, Lyly, *Works*, ii, line 371.

18 U. Ellis-Fermor, "Marlowe and Greene", *Studies in Honor of T. W. Baldwin*, ed. D. C. Allen (Urbana, 1958), p. 141.

Index